Advance Praise for *Writing Flash*

"In *Writing Flash*, Fred White has compiled a wonderfully compact resource for writers."
—from the Foreword by **Chris Tusa**, author of *The Yellow Girl*

"There is more to Flash than just its brevity, and White provides discerning writers with many lenses through which to understand and explore the diverse range and multiple styles of Flash. This insightful text, a welcome contribution, captures the essence of this important genre."
—**Opal Palmer Adisa**, author of *Love's Promise*

"This is a thoughtful book that covers flash fiction from Aesop to podcasts. White analyzes his own writing as well as others' to find those quintessential elements of storytelling that may particularly shine in abbreviated form."
—**Hannah Voskuil**, author of *Horus and the Curse of Everlasting Regret*

WRITING FLASH

How to Craft and Publish Flash Fiction for a Booming Market

Fred D. White

Fresno, California

Writing Flash

Published by Quill Driver Books
An imprint of Linden Publishing
2006 South Mary Street, Fresno, California 93721
(559) 233-6633 / (800) 345-4447
QuillDriverBooks.com

ISBN 978-1-61035-317-5

135798642

Printed in the United States of America
on acid-free paper.

Library of Congress Cataloging-in-Publication Data on file.

This book is for
Leonard and Teresa George
Steve and Lisa Mackay
Terry and Sue Tarrach
Frank Vozak and Terrie Rymer
Dear and steadfast friends;
and, of course, Therese

"I have written this letter longer than usual because I did not have the time to make it shorter."

—Blaise Pascal

"Brevity is the soul of wit."

—William Shakespeare

Other Books by Fred D. White

from Quill Driver Books:
LifeWriting: Drawing from Personal Experience to Create Features You Can Publish

from other publishers:
The Writer's Idea Thesaurus
Where Do You Get Your Ideas?
The Daily Reader
The Daily Writer
Approaching Emily Dickinson
Communicating Technology
Science and the Human Spirit
The Writer's Art

with Simone Billings:
The Well-Crafted Argument: A Guide and Reader, 6th Edition

as editor:
Essential Muir: A Selection of John Muir's Best Writings

Contents

Acknowledgments

I wish to thank Opal Palmer Adisa, Peter Cherches, Utahna Faith, Sherrie Flick, Anna Lea Jancewicz, Maria Negroni, Antonya Nelson, Lex Williford, and Hannah Bottomy Voskuil for permission to reprint their stories.

I also wish to thank the following individuals for their support and encouragement:

- My agent, Rita Rosenkranz, of the Rita Rosenkranz Literary Agency, NYC
- Kent Sorsky, publisher, Linden Publishing/Quill Driver Books
- My wife, Therese Weyna, for her wise suggestions

Foreword

In *Writing Flash*, Fred White has compiled a wonderfully compact resource for writers. As a writer who teaches flash fiction at the university level, I often find myself looking for a writing guide that not only provides writing exercises, strategies and techniques but that also includes a wealth of vital resources for writers. Because my students generally experiment with other forms, I always find myself looking for a writing guide that not only defines flash fiction effectively but one that also examines the connection between flash and longer, more traditional forms of fiction.

I was particularly delighted (as I think you will be) to find that, unlike most writing guides, *Writing Flash* not only examines the origins of flash fiction, tracing its beginnings to Old and New Testament parables (including ancient myths, allegories, sketches, and fairy tales), but it also explores the connection between flash, short stories, novellas, and novels. Sections like "The Influence of the Short Story on Flash Fiction" and "Writing Flash as Preparation for Writing Traditional Short Stories and Novels" are extremely rare in writing guides, and for that reason are uniquely useful and informative here.

Like many effective guides, *Writing Flash* provides sample flash stories for analysis, examining specific aspects (narrative voice, engagement, characters, and purpose) of each story. Not surprisingly, it also includes resources, such as a flash fiction checklist, information concerning query and cover letters, and a list of major writing contests (for individual stories and book-length collections). Most guides end here, but what's particularly striking and unique about *Writing Flash* is that it also focuses on various forms of flash fiction. Chapters such as "Writing Genre Flash Fiction,"

"Writing Literary Flash Fiction," "Writing Humorous or Satirical Flash Fiction," and "Writing Experimental Flash Fiction" provide readers with a unique insight into different forms of flash—a topic that is often overlooked in most flash guides.

But it doesn't stop there. *Writing Flash* moves beyond the act of writing itself, dedicating an entire chapter to preparing a volume of flash fiction, instructing writers on how to arrange and sequence the stories within the manuscript, even focusing on the use of intriguing titles for your stories and how those titles might warrant a particular arrangement. Readers will also be pleasantly surprised (as I was) that White devotes an entire chapter to marketing your work, detailing how writers can successfully build an audience through social media and participation in writing groups. As someone who has read numerous flash fiction writing guides, I can attest that most (if not all) books rarely touch upon marketing your work.

Yet, with all of this said, what's perhaps most notable about *Writing Flash* is how uniquely personal it is. Unlike many writing guides, White includes samples of his own work, analyzing each story as well as including interesting, personal asides relating to what inspired him to write the story, and what specific decisions he made while constructing the narrative. This tendency toward creating a uniquely intimate experience between reader and writer culminates nicely in Chapter 10 with the Self-Interview, where White personally answers common questions concerning how to successfully compress language, the reason for flash fiction's recent popularity, as well as what inspired White to write the book.

—Chris Tusa
Editor, *Fiction Southeast*
Author of *The Yellow Girl*

Part One

The Foundations of Flash

1

Introduction

Flash fiction is hot.* A hybrid and fluid genre, it has the narrative grip of traditional short fiction combined with the compression, imagery, allusiveness, and evocative power of poetry. A good flash tale instantly intrigues us, may also momentarily bewilder us, and delivers an emotional jolt to the solar plexus—all within one to four pages. It leaves us with the sense that a dark, overlooked corner of this world (or some other world) has been glimpsed, a place at once familiar and strange. Flashes are fun to write because they challenge us as writers to render a substantive drama with the fewest words possible. That means you must be able to convey characters, settings, and situations in a way that suggests much more than what you lay out on the surface. Don't let the shortness of flash stories mislead you into thinking that they're easy to write; like poems, they're easy to write badly. A successful flash story has all the aesthetic complexity of a story ten times its length. How can that be?

In this book, I will break down that aesthetic complexity into easily digestible lessons about the craft of flash writing so that you will be better able to master them. You first learn about the techniques of indirection: unfolding a story in a way that suggests much more than what is conveyed on the surface. You will learn to use literary tools like metaphor, symbolism, and allusion as strategies for creating stories that seem much more developed than their length would suggest. To ensure mastery of these and other nitty-gritty literary techniques, you will be asked to complete challenging but fun-to-do exercises along the way—exercises that will make you a stronger writer.

---

* Portions of Chapters 1 and 2 first appeared in my article "Flash Forward" (*Writer's Digest*, March/April, 2017).

The Basics of Flash Fiction

Before we get down to the nitty-gritty of crafting flash fiction, let's go over the basics. At the outset, I'm tempted to say that there *are* no basics to flash fiction. There are so many different varieties it seems purposeless to scrounge for universal elements aside from length (1,000 words or fewer is the generally accepted maximum length of a flash story, but some editors will accept slightly longer maximum lengths). Even so, we can make a few generalizations. First, flash stories are *stories* in the sense that some external or internal problem or struggle is brought into focus, and that one or more characters are involved, including the narrator. The problem is then resolved, or a new insight is gained into the problem.

Second, along with story, there is story compression. In other words, all the elements of a conventional length story are present (or implied) in a flash story, but they're compressed by allusion, indirection, innuendo, and metaphorical language that can evoke several things at once. To put it another way, instead of delineating setting, circumstance, and complex character behavior over many pages, the flash writer must allude to that complexity with "loaded" words and choice, precision-worded sentences or dialogue exchanges that imply a bigger picture.

As we shall see, these basics can be stretched and amplified and reshaped into all sorts of variations. Flash fiction, like poetry, invites innovation. At the same time, it has, over the few decades of its modern incarnation, produced a distinguished body of literature in its own right, as the works listed in the References section at the back of the book will attest.

Origins of Flash Fiction I: Parable, Fable, Fairy Tale, Allegory

What we call flash fiction today has been around, under different names, since ancient times. We can trace its roots to Old and New Testament parables like the Parable of the Potter in Jeremiah 18:1–10 and the Parable of the Sower in the Gospels (Matthew 13:1–23; Mark 4:3–9), and to fables (think of the fables of Aesop or La Fontaine) and myths. Fairy tales and their cousins, the folktales, grew out of these predecessors.

Here, for example, is one of Aesop's fables:

The Farmer and the Stork

by Aesop

A farmer placed nets on his newly-sown plowlands and caught a number of cranes, which came to pick up his seed. With them he trapped a stork that

> had fractured his leg in the net and was earnestly beseeching the farmer to spare his life. "Pray save me, Master," he said, "and let me go free this once. My broken limb should excite your pity. Besides, I am no crane, I am a stork, a bird of excellent character; and see how I love and slave for my father and mother. Look too at my feathers—they are not the least like those of a crane." The farmer laughed aloud and said, "It may be all as you say, I only know this: I have taken you with these robbers, the cranes, and you must die in their company."
>
> Birds of a feather flock together.
>
> —from FairyTalesCollection.com

In a mere 145 words, Aesop has created a dramatic situation that keeps us reading to the end. Will the captured stork argue his case convincingly enough to save his life? Is his argument a valid one? Does the farmer's counterargument—his verdict—falsify the crane's? The tagged-on moral vindicates the farmer's decision. Every sentence in the fable builds steadily upon the situation. It is this degree of unity that fables share with flash tales.

Many flash fiction writers continue to write modern-day parables, fables, and fairy tales and allegories. For example, in a flash parable titled "Dream #6" by the Egyptian author Naguib Mahfouz, winner of the 1988 Nobel Prize for Literature, one of the narrator's teachers returns from heaven after forty years to give his former pupil a folder containing corrections to the mistakes in his teachings.

Another example, this one cast as a modern fairy tale, is "The Blue Jar," by the Danish writer Isak Dinesen (famous for her memoir *Out of Africa*). This flash story, from Dinesen's collection *Winter's Tales* (1942), even opens like a fairy tale: "There was once an immensely rich old Englishman who had once been a courtier to the Queen and who now . . . cared for nothing but collecting ancient blue china." The Englishman's daughter, the Lady Helena, breaks away from the entrapments of royalty to continue her father's sailing adventures, and to pursue her lifelong quest to find precious pieces of ancient china possessed of a very rare shade of blue. We are soon caught up in Lady Helena's mystical vision of reality symbolized by that elusive shade of blue. In a mere thousand words, Dinesen immerses us in an alternate universe of uncanny beauty and human destiny.

Allegories are fairy-tale-like in the way characters or objects literally embody abstractions—think of John Bunyan's *The Pilgrim's Progress* (1687), in which Obstinacy, Sloth, Presumption, Envy, etc., are flesh-and-blood persons who obstruct the struggle of the protagonist, Christian, from achieving his goal of reaching the Celestial City. The allegory can still today serve as a template for morality tales.

I like to think of modern-day parables, fables, fairy tales, and allegories as flash morality tales because their concentrated nature allows their themes to shine through; but unlike many fables, such as Aesop's Fables, their themes or "morals" are not explicitly stated. Quite the contrary, the themes of many flash tales are only implicit, subject to reader interpretation.

These short tales take an abstract and complex concept (usually one that is theological or philosophical—but could also be scientific or psychological) and illustrates it in a dramatic, entertaining manner so that the truth can be readily understood and appreciated.

Origins of Flash Fiction II: The Sketch

Another cousin of flash fiction is the sketch, a snapshot of daily life, often humorous, witty, light-hearted, or satirical. Sketches can be in prose, fictional or nonfictional, or be rendered in play format. Classic examples include the *Salmagundi Papers* (1807) by Washington Irving (under his pseudonym Jonathan Oldstyle, Gentleman); *Sketches by Boz* (1836), the first published book by Charles Dickens—a collection of his sketches for the London *Morning Chronicle*; several of Mark Twain's humor pieces, collected in *The Celebrated Jumping Frog of Calaveras County and Other Sketches* (1867), and *Sketches, New and Old* (1875); and Langston Hughes's "Simple" sketches, written originally for an African-American newspaper and collected in the volumes *Simple Speaks His Mind* (1950), *The Best of Simple* (1961), and *Simple's Uncle Sam* (1963). A contemporary example of the humorous or satirical sketch is the weekly "Shouts & Murmurs" feature in *The New Yorker* magazine.

For advice on how to compose humorous and satirical flash fiction, see Chapter 6.

The Influence of the Short Story on Flash Fiction

The traditional short story has influenced the development of flash fiction from parable, fairy tale, or sketch to an independent genre. The short story sought, in the words of its earliest theorist, Edgar Allan Poe, to distinguish itself from the novel by limiting itself to a single, unified effect. In his review of Nathaniel Hawthorne's *Twice-Told Tales*, Poe characterized the short story writer as one who has "conceived, with deliberate care, a certain unique or single effect to be wrought out," and then "combines such events as may best aid him in establishing this preconceived effect." Furthermore, if the very first sentence does not bring about this effect, "then he has failed in his first step." For Poe, nothing in the story should diverge from this design. Flash fiction takes Poe's unified effect principle one step further: by virtue of its extreme brevity, the flash tale needs to strike the reader with a singular knockout punch—a single effect on steroids!

Writing Flash as Preparation for Writing Traditional Short Stories and Novels

This may sound a bit contradictory after I've pointed out that flash fiction is complex, and writing it takes considerable skill; but it is nevertheless true that learning to write this highly concentrated mode of fiction is excellent training for writing long fiction. It may seem that in longer fiction a writer can "spread things out" in a more casual manner. In truth, compression and complexity are just as important in long fiction, including novels, as they are in flash fiction. Longer fiction allows for a greater number of character interactions, more complex interactions, and more fully rendered settings and plot progressions (and regressions). I would argue that the skill you acquire from rendering significant detail in flash fiction will enrich your long story or novel greatly.

While I'm on the subject of longer fiction, it is interesting to note that some flash fiction writers have learned to have their novel cake and eat it too by writing their novels as a series of flash episodes, each able to stand on its own, yet together forming a coherent narrative. A good example of this is Zachary Mason's novel *The Lost Books of the Odyssey* (2010), consisting of 44 episodes, most of them flash length, depicting untold adventures of Odysseus. Another memorable example is Alan Lightman's 1993 best-seller *Einstein's Dreams*, each of the thirty episodes being an imagined dream Einstein has about the possible nature of time (e.g., "Suppose time is a circle, bending back on itself"; "There is a place where time stands still. Raindrops hang motionless in the air.")

Shaping a Flash Tale: A Quick Overview

There is no one entirely satisfactory definition of flash fiction because, like poetry, the genre keeps evolving in a dozen directions at once. Some flash fiction writers model their stories after parables; others experiment by creating text-image collages; still others experiment with unusual view-point characters. Bruce Holland Rogers, for example, has written a flash tale from the point of view of an infant trying to make sense of the world: "The dog's nose is here, then it is not, then it is here again. Voices come and go . . . He invents a language that contains all of his awareness . . . *Aglaglagl*." That last "word" happens to be the title of the story, which appears in the anthology *Flash Fiction Forward* (Norton, 2006).

In Chapters 4–7, I will take you through a step-by-step procedure for writing each kind of flash tale; but for now, let me introduce a basic set of guideline. To get started, imagine a scenario in which an adolescent or adult protagonist is confronted with a problem, struggles to resolve the problem, and experiences a significant change or revelation (epiphany) as a result of that struggle.

First, brainstorm

Don't go with the first thing that enters your mind; instead, conjure up several potential situations or predicaments and choose the best one. Let's say you jotted down a dozen of them, and then narrowed it to the following three:

- While shopping, a woman spots a man who resembles her dead husband and, despite her better judgment, starts following him.
- A young man becomes enamored with a woman who literally casts a spell over him, compelling him to do things against his nature.
- While examining an ancient burial site, an archaeologist feels an alien presence taking over her consciousness.

Next, determine the story premise in a synopsis

Establish your story premise in a one-paragraph synopsis. Let's shape a synopsis for each of the above potential situations:

- Maureen followed the man into the sporting goods store—the very one her husband went to when he needed new golf clubs. *This is insane*, she kept repeating to herself as she moved closer to him so she could see his face more clearly.

  (What happens next? Does the man notice her? If so, how does he react?)

- The dark-haired woman in the hotel lobby looked up from her magazine and gazed at me so intently that I stopped in my tracks. Even though I had never seen her before in my life, I felt as though we were somehow connected.

  (Is she a reporter? A fan? Her identity could suggest something about the narrator's profession.)

- First, the wall of the ground surrounding the dig seemed to soften; then it yawned open. Dr. Barton lurched back, gasping. Working long hours in the brutal Outback can induce hallucinations, but this was no hallucination.

  (Was her reaction psychosomatic? Had she chanced upon an ancient cult with magical powers that were still viable?)

Notice in each case how character and setting are molded simultaneously with the situation, all within the space of one or two sentences. This is what is meant by compression.

Now, draft the story

As you write the story, remember to include the three elements (listed below) needed to make reading the story a worthwhile experience:

- An intriguing way in which the protagonist has grappled with the problem. For example, Maureen's longing for her dead husband leads her to interrogate the man as if he really were her husband, who'd staged his death for whatever reason.
- The lesson learned or the epiphany experienced from the struggle; for example, something the man says to her helps her accept the painful reality of her husband's demise.
- The story milieu, evoked through vivid sensory details; for example, items in the sporting goods store generate memories about Maureen's husband that bring her grief to the point where she breaks down (catharsis).

Read the story aloud

You can gain additional insight into the strengths and shortcomings of your story by reading it aloud—even to yourself (if you can overlook sounding silly by doing so). Clunky sentences will sound even clunkier; lapses in continuity will likely become more conspicuous, as will gaps or inconsistencies in story development.

Take a break

Set the draft aside in order to gain artistic distance from it. Shift your attention to another creative endeavor. This hiatus will allow you to gain needed objectivity that will help you detect whatever flaws the story may still have.

Revise

I cannot overemphasize the importance of revising your stories. It has been my experience that stories do not come out finished the first time, very rarely after one rewrite, occasionally after two rewrites, and most commonly after three. Some of my stories I never got right until the fifth or sixth rewrite.

In Chapters 4–7, I will suggest revision strategies for particular kinds of flash fiction. But here, I'd like to lay out a few general principles:

- Think of revising as re-*seeing* the story (which is what re-vision actually means) instead of correcting or polishing (although those matters will most likely need addressing as well). This is especially relevant to flash fiction. One can tell a story from many perspectives, using many styles and points of view. Because the whole of a very brief story can be grasped with relative ease, try writing your story in several different ways.
- After finishing a draft, go on to something else. An interval of a day or two will help you view the draft more objectively, more critically.
- With each draft, ask yourself these questions:
    1. Is this the best possible way to tell this story? It may seem like it is after you've completed the draft, but believe me, it's an illusion. Don't be hasty in judging your work to be finished.
    2. What else can I do to strengthen the story's impact? Read through the draft at least three times to best answer this question: one to consider the actions and reactions of the characters; two to consider details: appearances, sensations, actions; three to consider story progression.
    3. Have I used the most precise word choice, sentence structure, and paragraph structure?
    4. Do I need to add or delete anything to strengthen the story? A weak or extraneous description or dialogue exchange can dramatically weaken a flash tale.

No one says you have to follow these steps in the order presented above. I've often plunged into a rough (or "discovery") draft, and used that draft to arrive at a story premise. And *then* I engage in brainstorming, focusing exclusively on that premise.

Randall Brown, author of the flash fiction collection *Mad to Live* (Flume Press, 2008), states that the principal demand of flash is "to find in compression what cannot be found otherwise." I think this is a crucial point: a flash story isn't merely a hyper-compressed regular-length story; rather, the compression (which, remember, is achieved by the skillful use of imagery and allusion) unlocks a dimension of experience that eludes us in other modes of creative expression.

In the words of Deb Olin Unferth, whose flash fiction collection *Minor Robberies* was published by McSweeney's in 2007, "Flash fiction is reckless daring." Merely daring to center a flash story on an offbeat or controversial idea or experience isn't enough: you have to have the courage to take risks with language and structure and tone of voice. In short, you have to deliver a swift literary punch to the reader's gut.

Resources for Flash Fiction Writers

I've discovered that a good way to be productive is to have a lot of reference materials at your fingertips. But let's not call them "reference materials"—think of them instead as "story-idea triggers." I'm not just talking about traditional staples like a hard-copy almanac, which is indispensable for accessing a zillion facts about the world and better than Googling (as web-surfing and hyperlinking, while useful for idea generation, can distract you from your original purpose). Many other reference works can prove to be treasure troves for generating ideas. Here are the ones that work for me:

- Anthologies of flash fiction: if you want to write flash masterfully, you've got to read flash obsessively. See the Further Reading section for a list of flash fiction anthologies and individual-author collections of flash fiction.

- Anthologies of myths, such as *Bullfinch's Mythology* or the beautifully illustrated *Myths: Tales of the Greek and Roman Gods* by Lucia Impelluso. And don't overlook a good mythological dictionary. My recommendation: *A Dictionary of Classical Mythology* by J. E. Zimmerman; it's thorough yet concise, has cross-references, pronunciation keys, and is inexpensive. Why mythology? These ancient tales are archetypal. They collectively capture the glories and follies of human behavior in the guise of gods and goddesses (and a lot of mortals to boot).

- A history of world art. I've discovered that images can instantly evoke story ideas.
- A dictionary of quotations.

Another Invaluable Resource: Your Writer's Notebook

Never slight the importance of keeping a notebook. Like the painter's sketchbook, it enables you to capture fleeting ideas before they're gone forever. Your notebook (not to be confused with a diary) is the place where you can be spontaneous, uninhibited, reckless, anything you want to be. Your notebook is for your eyes only. Out of this unfettered, unedited writing will come stories in embryonic form. Your notebook also keeps you writing regularly, fluently. The more you write, the more writing will become second nature to you.

I myself have filled dozens of pocket notebooks, not only with story ideas but complete drafts of flash stories, poems, scenes from plays, research notes, and bits of overheard conversation. I prefer to use a spiral notebook, one that fits into a pocket (or purse) so you can reach for it any time you get an idea. Some writers maintain a digital notebook as well, expanding their pocket-notebook jottings on screen.

Another point about notebook-keeping: it helps you to become a more astute observer. Remember that *everything* is potentially useful to a writer. So much of what one experiences in a given day—zillions of potential germs for stories—flits by unnoticed.

An excellent model for a writer's notebook is F. Scott Fitzgerald's. One section of *The Crack-Up*, the posthumously published collection of Fitzgerald's miscellaneous pieces, features excerpts from his notebooks, which he arranged alphabetically according to topic. Here are just a few of his notebook sections:

- Anecdotes
- Conversations and Things Overheard
- Ideas
- Moments (What People Do)
- Nonsense and Stray Phrases
- Scenes and Situations
- Titles

Now It's Time to Pick Up Your Pen

Practice is essential to learning to write well, so let's get started. I strongly recommend that you try your hand at every one of the following exercises. The same holds true for each and every exercise presented in subsequent chapters.

1. Develop and write a flash story.
    a. Take fifteen minutes or so to brainstorm for a flash story premise. Jot down whatever comes to mind, avoiding the temptation to reject anything that seems trivial. At the brainstorming stage, even trivial ideas can be tweaked into provocative ones.
    b. Choose one of the premises from your brainstorming session and work it into a one-paragraph synopsis that captures the potential story's opening situation, complication, and climactic moment.
    c. Expand your synopsis into a full-fledged first draft of the story. When finished, set it aside for a day, and then revise it. As mentioned earlier in the chapter, why not try reading it aloud? This can be very illuminating.
2. Choose any of the following quotations and write a one-sentence premise for a flash story based on it.
    a. Power is poison. (Henry Adams)
    b. It is a most miserable thing to feel ashamed of home. (Charles Dickens)
    c. I have always depended on the kindness of strangers. (Tennessee Williams)
    d. Much madness is divinest sense . . . Much sense the starkest madness. (Emily Dickinson)
    e. Ignorance and superstition bear a close relation to each other. (James Fenimore Cooper)
    f. Who could deceive a lover? [*Quis fallere posit amantem?*](Virgil)
    g. The world more often rewards outward signs of merit than merit itself. (La Rochefoucauld)
    h. Life imitates art more than art imitates life. (Oscar Wilde)

3. Draft a flash tale based on the synopsis you wrote for #2 above.

4. You probably remember from high school one of Robert Frost's most famous poems, "Stopping by Woods on a Snowy Evening": The narrator on his way to a village on horseback stops to admire the snowfall in the woods.

   My little horse must think it queer
   To stop without a farmhouse near

   Write a flash story about this man, who, despite his "promises to keep," allows himself to be charmed by the winter scene.

5. Prepare to write a flash allegory by doing the following:

   a. Write a description of how your allegory will work. For example, you might use an amusement park as an allegory for your main character's stages in life: merry go-round = childhood; roller-coaster = teen years, etc.

   b. Write a premise paragraph explaining your character's goal (e.g., what does he or she want most out of visiting the amusement park?)

   c. Draft the story.

6. After completing a couple dozen notebook entries, open a digital file and reproduce them according to category. To give you some idea of the kinds of categories to set up (which by the way will help you generate a greater variety of notebook entries!), review the partial list of entries on page 12 that F. Scott Fitzgerald used for his notebook. Consider creating a similar list for your own notebook.

7. In one page, dramatize a confrontation between two persons—say a police officer and someone he or she has pulled over; or two college-dorm roommates with very different personalities.

8. Turn the one-page exercise you wrote for #7 into a complete sketch (2–4 pages), with a distinct introductory scene, a complication, and a climax/resolution.

9. Adapt one of Aesop's fables to a modern-day situation. Here are a couple possibilities:

   a. The Boy Who Cried Wolf = The ET Conspiracy Theorist Who Cried Wolf. Possible premise: Everyone laughed at Clyde for insisting that aliens were invading his town; but then ETs actually decided to invade Clyde's town, knowing that he wouldn't be believed.

   b. The Wolf in Sheep's Clothing = The Tyrant King Who Disguised Himself as a Rebel. Possible Premise: During an uprising against the monarchy, the tyrant king tries to escape being lynched by disguising himself as one of the rebels; but one of the king's guards slays him when he catches the disguised king fleeing the palace.

10. Take a story or scene from (or inspired by) the Bible and give it a modern-day spin in a 500–1000-word flash tale. Here are a few ideas for you to work with:
    a. Moses returns from Mt. Sinai with the Ten Commandments.
    b. Astronaut returns from an interstellar voyage with an amazing message for humanity
    c. Jesus raises Lazarus from the dead.
    d. Archaeologists find the tomb and the remains of Alexander the Great, extract his DNA, and bring him back to life.
11. Write a modern flash tale based on of one of the following classics:
    a. *Little Red Riding Hood*: Possibility: A young policewoman disguises herself as a waif to lure a sexual predator into the open.
    b. *Frankenstein*: A scientist tries to clone himself, but his DNA gets mixed in with that of his pet Cocker Spaniel.
    c. *The Odyssey*: (Lots of options here) A modern-day Odysseus, who works for the CIA, is charmed by a Russian-spy-sorceress (Circe) who threatens to turn him into a pig if he doesn't hand over top secret files.

2

Exploring the Possibilities of Flash Fiction

As with long-form fiction or poetry, flash fiction can either be based on traditional models, or it can venture into new modes of storytelling. Because of its brevity, flash fiction is an ideal medium for innovation. I myself enjoy working within traditional genres, especially science fiction and fantasy. There is plenty of room, I discovered, for innovation within genres. On occasion, though, I like to experiment with style and structure. I suspect that deep inside every writer is the urge to break free of preconceptions, of conventions. Flash fiction is a good way to go rogue artistically.

In this chapter, I will introduce you to the different varieties of flash fiction to give you a sense of the range of its possibilities. In Chapter 3 I will focus on the techniques of analyzing flash stories in each of these categories, because analytical skills are an important means of augmenting creative skills. Then, in Chapters 4–7, I will take you through a step-by-step procedure for writing a flash story in each of those categories. Be sure that you complete at least some of the exercises at the end of each chapter. You will then be ready to submit your stories to journal editors for possible publication; Chapters 8 and 9 will show you exactly how to do that.

Literary Flash I: Character Emphasis

Describing a story as "literary" means that it is more concerned with conveying subtleties of human behavior in the context of a compelling predicament, employing time-honored literary devices like irony and symbolism—devices, by the way, that poets typically rely on. Indeed, the distinction between literary flash fiction and prose poetry is rather blurry.

Readers turn to literary fiction to gain insight into, and appreciation of, what it means to be human, how human beings can deal with adversity, how they're able to cope with the mistakes they've made. Literary flash fiction is no different, except that it aims to transmit its purpose in no more than 1000 words. It is, quite frankly, a daunting challenge—some might even argue that it's impossible.

The first question that likely springs to mind is, Why not use all the words one can to tell the story? What is so great about restricting the story's length to a thousand or fewer words? The answer is that the more concentrated something is, the more radiant it can be. Think of the element carbon: one of its manifestations is coal; another, the result of stupendous subterranean pressures, is diamond. A literary flash story dazzles readers with its ability to convey an insight into the human condition with carefully honed language and a limited but precise selection of detail. The trick is to use just enough details to *imply* what a longer story would make explicit.

Let's first consider the character-based literary flash story. Writers may wish to capture characters' individuality—their quirks and charms, their states of mind, the peculiar ways in which they struggle to make sense of their lives, and how they cope with or overcome the forces working against them. Consider the following literary flash tale:

All Girl Band

by Utahna Faith

My all girl band is in trouble. Not musical trouble, not financial trouble, not boy trouble, not even the trouble of looking like beautiful vampires every night and every day. We have simply done something wrong. We do not know what it is, and I am sure we did not mean to do it. Nevertheless, we are in trouble.

My father looks at me nervously. How can I be so white-skinned, ebony-haired, red-lipped and ethereal, when my mother, at my age with the same face and body, was suntanned, golden-haired, peach-lipped and earth-bound? I believe I made him nervous. Yes, I made him nervous, and it's about time.

I am back in our old house, bad house, in my old room, changing clothes. What does one wear to jail? I am frightened.

The other three "Four Whores of the Apocalypse" arrive and we console one another. As we walk through the family room past the loud football game, my father looks at us without moving his mouth or turning his head. As I say good-bye he nods once, chin down, hold a beat, chin level. That is all.

We climb into the red Ford Fairlane, slide our own CD into the player and sing. I know through the terror in my stomach that we have never been so on, so hot, so perfect.

Of course we are right to turn ourselves in.

—first appeared in *Café Irreal* #31; reprinted in *Flash Fiction Forward* (ed. James Thomas and Robert Shepard, 2006)

Uthana Faith has given us a three-dimensional protagonist, caught up in a situation both realistic and mystifying. Like many flash tales, it feels complete even though it's only 233 words long; yet more things are unexplained than explained. What did the narrator and her friends do that got them into trouble, and that made them decide to turn themselves in? We suspect that that isn't the point of the story. So what would be the point? The father's behavior toward his daughter gives us a strong clue: In a longer story, the conflict between father and daughter would have been rendered more fully. In flash fiction, however, indirection is a key part of the aesthetic.

Literary Flash II: Theme Emphasis

I mentioned in Chapter 1 that flash fiction has its roots in parables, fables, and fairy tales—ancient and medieval modes of storytelling that continue to this day—and flash fiction is an ideal embodiment for them, not only because of its compact mode of storytelling, but also because it can aim to convey an explicit theme or moral. That is to say, the characters, engaging and memorable as they might be, exist to highlight the moral precept or the deep philosophical or spiritual insight being dramatized.

Let's first go over the differences among two closely related modes of storytelling, the parable and allegory, followed by overviews of fables and fairy tales:

Parable or allegory

Theme- or moral-stressed. The characters may seem sketchy, generalized, and may not even be presented as individuals (e.g., "The people of the village thrived on superstition"). They exist solely to illustrate the author's insight into a moral or ethical conundrum. Franz Kafka, Jorge Luis Borges, and Italo Calvino are masters of the modern-day parable.

One distinction between a parable and an allegory is that in the latter, human traits—Greed, Ambition, Lust, Sloth, etc. serve as characters. The most famous novel-length allegory in English is John Bunyan's *The Pilgrim's Progress* (1687), a dream-vision in which the protagonist, Christian, struggles to reach the Celestial City, but first must get through obstacles like the

Slough of Despond. There are also philosophical allegories, such as Plato's Allegory of the Cave (from his *Republic*), in which the characters serve to illustrate a profound insight—in this case, into the relationship between reality and illusion.

Here is an example of a modern-day flash parable; it comes from the pen of an Argentine writer:

The Baby

by Maria Negroni; translated by Anne Twitty

> My baby is playing in the bath, delighted. I begin to wash his head and spend some time at this. Then he begins. When I start to rinse his hair, I can't find him. I turn around, and there he is again. I don't understand what is happening, and grow stern. I scold him. I don't like what he's doing. The baby laughs, more and more amused, glimmers for an instant and vanishes again. My impatience only makes things worse. He disappears more and more quickly, doesn't even give me time to protest. Through layers of uneasiness, I glimpse his mischievous glance; my blindness is his victory, my jealousy his passion. For a while, I go on resisting; I don't know how to welcome impotence. The baby just wants to play. The game is dazzling and lasts a lifetime.
>
> —first appeared in *Night Journey*, 2002; reprinted in *Flash Fiction International* (ed. James Thomas et al., 2015)

A fine demonstration of how much story can be concentrated into 200 words, "The Baby" dramatizes its theme, that children crave independence from their parents beginning even from infancy, with an air of whimsy, and ending with an almost Aesop-like ending that nevertheless does not seem tagged on like Aesop's fables.

Fable

Equal emphasis on theme and character. The characters are animals with distinctly human characteristics. Usually in very short works, the characters represent human types, as they do in allegories.

Fairy tale

Equal emphasis on theme and character. In fairy tales the characters tend to be more three-dimensional than in parables or allegories, sometimes capable of complex behavior and emotion. Fairy tales almost always involve magic and clear-cut distinctions between good and evil, hero and villain. Take for example the Grimm fairy tale "The Fisherman and His Wife": A fisherman who lives in poverty with his wife catches a flounder who begs for his life on grounds that he is a prince. Finding it amazing enough that the fish can speak, he returns it to the sea. But then he has to face his angry wife, who insists that he demand from the magical fish something in return for his good deed—namely a nicer house to replace the "pigsty" they're now living in. The fish agrees, and the fisherman returns to find his pigsty replaced by a large, charming cottage and a happier wife. But the wife's happiness is short-lived when she realizes that the fish could have granted her even more—namely a castle. When she gets the castle, she then wants to be King—then Emperor—then Pope, then godlike master of the sun and moon. Finally the flounder-prince tells the fisherman to return home "and you will find your wife back again in her pigsty."

The theme of this fairy tale, of course, is that greed is self-defeating. But the tale also captures the complex psychological reality of grappling with the tension between opportunity and exploitation. It is this kind of complexity that modern flash fiction often tries to capture. For example, one can imagine modern-day counterparts to the fisherman, his wife, and the flounder that might go something like this: A poor laborer who wins $1000 with a lottery ticket (the flounder counterpart being Lady Luck) secretly gives half the money to charity. But his wife, incensed that he didn't keep the whole prize, is so determined to get back the other $500 she spends even more than that on more lottery tickets—and loses it all.

Genre Flash Fiction

By "genre" I mean the traditional, market-based categories of fiction: romance, mystery, science fiction, fantasy, thriller, military, along with their numerous subdivisions (historical romance, epic fantasy, steampunk science fiction, espionage thriller, political thriller, etc.). "Genre" can also apply to target audience (juvenile, young adult, new adult). As book-consumer habits change, so do some of the sub-genre descriptions—but the tried and true major classifications of adult/ young adult/children's fiction and nonfiction will always stand firm. If your goal is to write commercial fiction in one or more of these categories, it helps to be familiar with what publishers and agents (hence readers) are expecting, and to restrict artistic innovation to within these expectations.

A genre flash story, like a long-form story, drops readers into a conflict situation that is characteristic of a mystery, romance, or some other recognizable scenario in which danger and/ or emotional turmoil looms. Your viewpoint character must struggle to solve the mystery, or resolve the romantic conundrum, or defuse the danger. He or she may or may not succeed, but by the end of the story, something must have changed.

As I mentioned earlier, it is possible to experiment (aside from abiding by publishers' constraints) within a traditional genre category. See if you can guess the genre (or combination of genres) in the following 800-word flash tale:

The Face in the Rock

by Fred D. White

They were necking in a thicket off the hiking trail. Delmore heard himself tell Jade that he wanted to spend the rest of his life with her, that he would do anything for her.

"You must promise."

"I promise."

She smiled, caressing his face. "Then your fate is sealed."

Despite being overwhelmed with longing for his raven-haired, jewel-eyed girlfriend, he felt vaguely unnerved by what she'd just said; but before he could move his lips, she said, "Come with me; I want to show you something."

Jade's blood-red lipstick was smeared; he wanted to kiss her again; he wanted to gaze forever into her luminous green eyes. "Sh-show me what?" he managed to say.

She smiled. "C'mon."

He followed her back to the trail. "Where are we going?"

"You'll see!" She started running.

He caught up to her and was tempted to tackle her to the ground and wrap her long legs around his neck; but she grinned as if reading his thoughts. "There will be plenty of time for that."

So she *was* reading his thoughts.

After a few moments she slowed down and said, "Don't be scared, okay?"

"Scared of what?"

She stopped in front of a large rock and placed both hands on it.

"What do you mean, 'Don't be scared'?"

"Just watch."

The rock's surface became translucent. Delmore rubbed his eyes as a holographic image materialized. He gasped when he realized it was his own face, although considerably older. This had to be some bizarre optical illusion. He glared at Jade. "What kind of sorcery is this?"

"I conjure up the future, Del. Some of us use crystal balls; I prefer rocks. Anyway, now that you have pledged yourself to me, you'll be able to see into the future too!"

Delmore shuddered at the sight of his face in the rock. "He seems—*I* seem—to be in distress."

Jade studied the face for a moment, her brow furrowing. "Hmmm . . . maybe your promise wasn't sincere after all."

He backed away from Jade, who now seemed *alien*. "What have you done to me?" He tried to read what was lurking behind her eyes, but all he could see was their haunting beauty that had turned his brain to mush.

"Delmore!" The voice came from the rock.

He leaned in closer. "Did you just call me?" He felt like a moron, speaking to a rock.

"Get rid of her or else she'll—" Jade suddenly did something with her hands and the face vanished.

Before he could ask her what had happened, she took off down the trail.

He was about to run after her when the face in the rock reappeared and spoke again: *"Find her, for God's sake; make her break the spell."*

"What *is* she?"

"A demon who feeds on the intense emotions of the men she captures and holds in her thrall. Now hold still so I can forge a mind-link with you."

"You're going to mind-link with me? With your earlier self?"

"It's our only chance to avoid eternal imprisonment."

There was a violent flash of light, and he staggered backwards.

"Now hurry!" said the voice of his future self inside his head.

He ran as fast as he dared down the trail, nearly twisting his ankle. "Jade!" he yelled. He forced himself to keep going until he reached the trail head.

No Jade.

Again he yelled. "Jade! Where are you?" It was growing dark.

And suddenly, there she was, shrouded in shadow in the picnic area.

"You can't resist me, can you?" she said, moving toward him, her luminous green eyes wide and predatory in the dim light.

"Don't come any closer."

She came closer. He ached to hold her in his arms again, to inhale the hypnotic fragrance of her hair . . .

She opened her arms and every inch of his body cried out to embrace her, to fall into her gravity well of indescribable pleasure.

But even as he hungered for the creature looming before him, the voice inside his head—his own voice from his future self—commanded him to attack. *"Grab her throat! Force her to break the spell, or you're a goner."*

"What if she refuses?"

"Do it!"

He leapt upon her, desperate to crush his mouth against hers, and to crush her windpipe at the same time. "Release me, Jade!" he and his future self simultaneously commanded.

She twisted violently out of his grip and clawed his face. His lust now overcome by panic, Delmore lunged for her once again and dug his thumbs into her throat. Searing pain knifed through his head, but he forced his thumbs into her windpipe and squeezed with all his might.

Jade writhed, and then went limp; she dropped lifeless to the ground.

"Idiot!" shrieked the voice inside his head. *"You were supposed to get her to break the spell first!"*

—first published in *Aphelion* Magazine, May, 2016. Web.

As you can see, my protagonist, Delmore, is faced with a be-careful-what-you-wish for situation. Succumb to the charms of a sorceress and your fate may be sealed in more ways than one! You may also have picked up overtones of dark humor; that was deliberate. Genre mixing can add sparkle to a flash tale. By the way, to answer the question I posed when introducing this story, I have combined romance, fantasy, and horror, with a dash of dark comedy.

If you find yourself leaning toward genre flash fiction, remember that there are still many possibilities for being innovative.

Humorous or Satirical Flash Fiction

It surprises me that there aren't more literary journals that publish satire or humor. They're out there, but you need to devote a good chunk of time to searching them out. My guess is that satire and humor writing resists blanket guidelines: what is funny to you might be offensive to me, and vice versa. Even so, I like to think that it's up to us writers to set a market trend—so, if you think you have a literary funny bone, go for it! Find some issue in current events that gets your dander up—but instead of venting steam with expletives, try writing a scenario that would transform your anger into literary wit. I will illustrate with a case-in-point of my own. A while back I got incensed over a politician who argued that classroom teachers should arm themselves. What next, I thought: children arming themselves too? I took out my notepad, started scribbling away, and eventually came up with this satirical flash skit:

Welcome to Kindergarten

by Fred D. White

The Welcome

MS. BLOCK: Welcome to Kindergarten, cadets! My name is Ms. Block, which is spelled [writes on overhead transparency] B-l-o-c-k, which rhymes with Glock [shows image of a Glock-17 handgun]. Meet your Protector.

It weighs just a teeny bit less than two pounds, and is really easy to hide inside your backpacks. Best of all, it comes with a 17-round magazine, which means that when the baddies come for you, you'll be able to discharge a whole bunch of bullets into them without having to stop to reload—and in just a few seconds too! Boy, will that make them think twice about being bad guys, RIGHT, CLASS?

CLASS: Right, Ms. Block!

MS. BLOCK: And of course, I too will be armed, just like all the other teachers here at Prince of Peace Elementary. You cadets will feel even safer here than at home, where your parents foolishly keep their Protectors out of your reach. Any questions? Yes, Timothy?

TIMOTHY: Uhm, do we get to play "Witches 'n' Wizards?"

MS. BLOCK: Timothy! Shame on you! Did you forget that witchcraft and magic are the tools of Satan?

The Drill

MS. BLOCK: Listen up, cadets. I have placed loaded Glock-17s inside each of your crayon boxes. I'm going to count to three, which is all the time you will have to grab your weapon if an assailant should blast his or her way into the classroom, brandishing an AR-17. Are you ready? On my mark . . . One! Two!—*Jared!* I did not say "Three" yet!

JARED: Sorry, Ms. Block.

MS. BLOCK: Just for that, you must stay after school and write "I promise to follow all safety protocols exactly as ordered" on the board twenty-five times. Bonnie, do you have a question?

BONNIE: Uhm, is it okay if I start shooting *before* the bad guys come into the room?

MS. BLOCK: Good question, sweetie. What do you think, Dylan?

DYLAN: Hmmm, what if it's not a bad guy trying to get in? You know—what if the principal wants to surprise us with some cookies or something?

ANNIE [leaping to her feet]: That is so lame, Dylan, you dork! The principal is part of the school's outer-perimeter line of defense.

DYLAN: Call me a dork again, Annie, and I'll rip off your braids and shove them down your ugly throat.

MS. BLOCK: Now, now, Dylan and Annie, have you forgotten your anti-bullying lessons? What do you say to each other?

ANNIE: I apologize, Dylan.

DYLAN: I apologize, Annie. I will never, ever call you a bad name again.

MS. BLOCK: That's better. Besides, you should know by now that our interim principal, General Lyons (and may our last principal rest in peace), is no cookie fairy.

The Discharge

MS. BLOCK: And now, cadets, our temporary principal and former Brigadier General, Ozzie Lyons, wants to say a few words to you.

LYONS: Ahem. Young combatants, let me first congratulate you on the successful completion of the first stage of your para-military training. It is something you will value even more than readin', writin', and 'rithmetic! Don't get me wrong; them three R's are important, but what good are they if you're a bloody, bullet-shredded corpse, right? [He guffaws.]

Now it is my honor to dispatch you to First Grade, where you will be introduced to advanced military weaponry, including grenade launchers, M16s, Heckler and Koch submachine guns, L42A1 sniper rifles, and a whole lot more. I won't say any more about them, knowing how much fun it is to be surprised by brand new toys. And now . . . TEN-SHUN! [All the children leap to attention.] Ms. Block will call each of you up to the front of the class to receive your honorable kindergarten discharge and your own very first box of ammo.

The Sing-Along

MS. BLOCK: Let us all sing together, cadets, to celebrate our freedom as red-blooded young Americans. General Lyons, please set up your camcorder so you can shoot this joyous moment for posting on our respective Facebook pages.

[LYONS reaches for his duffel bag—several of the children fling open their desks and reach for their crayon boxes—then, laughing, close up their desks. LYONS begins shooting the video.]

MS. BLOCK: Everyone ready? a-one, a-two, a-three . . .

THE CHILDREN:

We are the good guys, the bold white-Hatters—
The first responders, when bad guys slay.
We'll take 'em out fast—their brains will splatter;
So please don't take our weapons away.

—first published in *Pidgeonholes* vol. 2, (April–June 2015)

I should tell you that, when it comes to controversial issues like carrying guns, some editors will shy away from publishing satires that have what they consider to be "a political agenda"—which was the reason one editor gave me for rejecting the piece.

And what of my mixing of literary genres like drama and poetry. Is that really acceptable? Answer: of course! And even if it weren't . . . hey, you're the artist in charge. Do your own thing—just make it reflect your best writing so that it resonates with readers—at least with some of them.

Experimental Flash Fiction

Some flash stories do not resemble conventional short stories; rather they seem more like poems or some hybrid genre. As with any art form, innovation is part of its essence, always seeking new ways to make language embrace the human condition and the nature of reality.

In Chapter 7, I will lay out several suggestions for experimenting with flash fiction. For now, let's look at some of the varieties of experimental flash fiction that are out there. In addition to experiments with extreme brevity (e.g., Haiku-like six-word stories; micro-flash stories of 25–250 words), flash writers experiment with subject matter, point of view, stream-of-consciousness, language and style, and even formatting and mixed-media (photographs, drawings, and other visual elements). Regardless of how you experiment, though, your ultimate goal should be reader delight and/or edification.

To whet your appetite, consider this peculiarly rendered tale with its all-too-familiar theme.

7:23 P.M.

by Sherrie Flick

Paint your nails. Inhale. Exhale slowly. Let the paint dry.

It's easy. This waiting.

Once the nails are dry, do the dishes. Slowly, deliberately. Dry each plate, each cup, each bowl. Close each cabinet door without letting it make a noise. Inhale.

Vacuum straight lines in the carpet. Dust with the kind of precision your mother would be proud of. Exhale.

Think, think, think.

Check the machine for messages. When the solid red light is still solid and red, put your hands on your hips. Look up. Keep looking. Stand that way until your whole life clings to itself and settles at the base of your spine.

Take a shower. Exhale.

Look at yourself in the mirror. Suck in your stomach. Stick it out as far as it will go. Get dressed.

Imagine the phone will ring the minute you make yourself rush out the door.

Rush out the door.

As you walk to the bus stop, recreate the message word for word. It ends with love and a soft click.

Wait for your bus. Look up the street and down. See hope in the stoplight, the car alarm, the corner deli's lighted sign. Watch the bus come screaming in.

Let it leave the curb without you. Let it pull away.

Squint. Raise your hand to your eyes.

Wait for the next and the next and the next.

—from *I Call This Flirting*; Flume Press, 2004

Sherrie Flick skillfully uses short, sometimes fragmentary, sentences and paragraphs to capture the narrator's anxiety and obsessive temperament, bordering on neurosis. Every minute of her life is an entrapment within that minute (hence the title).

Now It's Time to Pick Up Your Pen

1. Even if you're determined to write a certain kind of flash fiction, I urge you to try your hand at all the different kinds described in this chapter. Here's how you can have fun doing that:
   - Write a one-sentence premise for each of the five main types of genre flash (romance, mystery/thriller, science fiction, fantasy, horror), literary flash, humor/satire flash, experimental flash—a total of eight story premises.
   - Choose one of the above premises and expand it into a one-paragraph synopsis.
   - Draft the story.
   - Repeat the above steps for any or all of the other premises.
2. The daily newspaper is fine source for potential flash stories. Go through today's paper and write a one-sentence story premise for five different news stories and editorials you come across. Oh, and don't forget the business, sports, food, and entertainment sections!

Example

News Story	Possible Flash Story Premise
Opioid users fill jails, but rarely get treated.	Correctional officer battles status quo in wanting to help opioid addicts overcome their addiction rather than jail them.

80-year-old gymnast amazes fans.	An octogenarian grandmother, inspired by the story of an 80-year-old gymnast, decides to train for a marathon, despite her doctor's warnings.

3. Start preparations for a cross-genre flash story with a historical setting—for example a mystery flash in which a famous person serves as sleuth (Edgar Allan Poe attempting to solve the mystery of a close friend's disappearance; Socrates attempting to find out who is poisoning his students); or a love story between an Egyptian slave and a priestess. Your first step will be to research the historical background carefully. Who were Poe's friends, and how important were they to his personal and professional life? Why would anyone want to poison Socrates' students? We know, through Plato, that he was found guilty of corrupting students with his teachings and sentenced to suicide; perhaps one of his students dared to promulgate some of Socrates' more controversial teachings. Once you have completed these preparations, write the story.
4. Try experimenting with different ways of narrating a flash tale. For example, you might tell the love story of the Egyptian priestess and the slave through separate interior monologues—first the slave's, then the priestess's; or you might organize the story through three or four clandestine meetings, or through secret messages, recruiting the assistance of a secret messenger.
5. Writers sometimes are motivated by what stirs them up emotionally, what tugs at their heartstrings, what angers them. Start keeping a list of events, attitudes, and behaviors that trigger a strong emotional response. Every so often, peruse this list and choose one or more items for a flash story.
6. Ready to try your hand at satire? Start by jotting down incidents from current events that seem ripe for satirical treatment, such as bad behavior by well-known public figures; double standards in policy-making; or cliché-ridden TV shows. Choose the one incident that seems most susceptible to satirical treatment—e.g., to being exposed, in a comic manner, to ridicule. Next, capture the satirical situation in

a single paragraph. Finally, expand the paragraph into a flash satire between 500 and 1000 words.

7. Take a famous fairy tale, such as "Little Red Riding Hood," "Cinderella," or "Hansel and Gretel," and retell it in a modern-day context as a 500–1000 word flash tale. For example, you might think of Little Red Riding Hood as a young inner-city girl who faces danger every time she visits her grandmother's apartment across town.

3

Analyzing Flash Fiction

Good writers need to be good readers. My definition of a good reader is one who understands and appreciates the techniques authors use to compose their stories. In this chapter, we'll examine the workings of each type of flash story described in Chapter 2, using tools of analysis that will come in handy when you apply them to your own fiction writing. Like any other art form, fiction thrives on inventiveness and risk-taking, and flash fiction is especially amenable to such creative daring. But even the most inventive writers rely on basic techniques.

Being able to analyze a story is important for several reasons. First, it helps you become a better critic of your own work. You might have become aware in your earliest fiction writing efforts of the gulf between your stories and those that you read in print. Eventually, as you study the craft, that gulf shrinks. The turning point may come for you, as it did for me, when you find yourself saying, "I can write as good a story as that!" or even "I can do better than that!"

The Criteria for Analyzing Flash Fiction

Before we analyze examples of the several subgenres of flash fiction, let's review the criteria that will be informing our analysis. These criteria are relevant to the full range of flash fiction, regardless of type.

Story-ness: Is there a story here? "Story-ness" doesn't necessarily mean a genre-fiction type plot; i.e., it need not adhere to a classic problem-complication-climax-resolution structure. Those elements can be hinted at, but there should at least be some sense of conflict, malaise, or foreboding.

Immediate engagement: A flash story should grab the reader's attention instantly, either with a strangely worded sentence, or the depiction of something unusual, or a dialogue exchange that startles, or only starts making sense as the story unfolds.

Distinctive narrative voice: The narrator should possess a distinctive personality and/or a distinctive way of perceiving the world, by way of his narrative voice. Think of Huck Finn introducing himself: "You don't know me without you have read a book by the name of *The Adventures of Tom Sawyer*; but that ain't no matter."

Authentic characters: The people in the story can be peculiar, menacing, or enigmatic but should still come across as believable, identifiable. This is important because authenticicity enables the reader to suspend disbelief.

Purpose: Stories should always be about something worthwhile, even if that main idea emerges indirectly.

Analysis of a Literary Flash Story*

Let's take a close look at a flash story, one of my own, which first appeared in the October 2013 issue of *Burningword Literary Journal*. We're going to analyze this piece in several stages. First read the story quickly, non-critically; next, read it again, this time paying attention to how it's put together; read it a third time for voice, word choice, paragraphing, and use of dialogue. Finally, study the analysis that follows to see how closely it comes to your own. I suppose I should warn you that one of the characters uses disturbingly rough language; but I think you'll agree such language is necessary for conveying this particular character's nature.

The Confession
by Fred D. White

"I know that Cheri's been cheating on me."

I looked at Rod. We were jogging together around the lake. "She told you?"

"Hell no; the bitch is too afraid of me to spit it out."

"Then how—"

"Her *face* told me. I been with her long enough to tell. No different than if she confessed outright." Rod picked up speed; I managed to keep up with him even though I hadn't been jogging much lately.

"Maybe you're misreading her. Maybe—"

*An earlier version of this section appeared in my article "Flash Forward," *Writer's Digest*, March/April 2017.

"Here's what I'm gonna do to the bastard once I squeeze it out of her who she screwed." He slowed down and pulled a switchblade from his shorts pocket. "I'm gonna cut off his dick. Slowly, so I can enjoy the screaming. Then I'll shut him up by shoving it into his mouth. And then I'll grab my .38 and—"

"Jesus, Rod, stop it. Just stop it!"

"It'll be quite a show, Gus. I'll give you a ringside seat. 'Wild West Justice.'"

We finished our jog in silence. As I turned to head for home, Rod said, "If she's still visiting with Jill tell her to get her ass back here *now*."

Jill and Cheri were on the sofa, solemnly watching Cheri's son, Rod Jr., playing with the puppy. I pecked Jill on the cheek. She didn't respond.

Cheri stared at me; then she said, "Did you and Rod have a good run?"

"I need a drink," I said—more to myself than to Jill or Cheri, and went into the kitchen. I poured some whiskey into a tumbler, took a gulp, sat down, and put my head in my hands.

Cheri walked in after a decent interval. She looked ill. I could see what she was thinking.

—first appeared in *Burningword Literary Journal* 68 (Oct. 2013). Web.

Analysis

Story-ness: "The Confession" builds around a predicament involving the narrator (Gus), his adversary who also happens to be a friend (Rod), Rod's wife (Cheri), and Gus's wife (Jill). The story unfolds in two settings (the lake, where Rod and Gus are jogging, and afterwards in Gus's home).

Immediate engagement: The opening dialogue immediately introduces the predicament:

> "I know that Cheri's been cheating on me."

A note on flash fiction compression: Notice how I use dialogue to simultaneously establish the predicament and to establish the characters' natures:

> I looked at Rod. "She told you?"
> "Hell no; the bitch is too afraid of me to spit it out."

Rod's crude reference to his wife suggests a troubled marriage, that Rod treats her in a way that makes her afraid of him. Might that be Cheri's reason for cheating? By the way, names can carry symbolic weight. I chose "Cheri," for example, because it sounds like "cherish"—an ironic counterpoint to Rod's attitude toward her. I then wanted to drop a hint that Gus is the one having the affair with Rod's wife, but without giving away the ending:

> Rod picked up speed; I managed to keep up with him even though I hadn't been jogging much lately.

Authentic characters: It is a fiction writer's job to present the characters as authentic persons in the way they talk and act and react. Gus understandably starts to worry that Rod did more than see the confession in Cheri's face; that he might finally have forced her to confess outright:

> "Maybe you're misreading her. Maybe—

Rod then interrupts him with his vile mutilation scenario—a further clue that he suspects Gus, and therefore wants to frighten him. Gus's reaction—"Jesus, Rod, stop it. Just stop it!"—shows that Rod has shaken him to the core, exactly what Rod intended to do, presumably. This possibility is reinforced in the next passage:

> "It'll be quite a show, Gus. I'll give you a ringside seat."

Distinctive narrative voice: I wanted to use the narrative voice to convey foreboding. Thus, when Gus returns home he sees Cheri with Gus's wife, Jill, on the sofa, watching Rod Jr. playing with the puppy. They are not merely watching the boy, they are *solemnly* watching him. In flash fiction, you can make a single word suggest a great deal—that Cheri had confessed to Jill, that Cheri could no longer live with her guilt, that Jill felt her trust in Gus crumble away.

More compression: to add another reason behind Gus's indiscretion, I showed Rod Jr. playing with Jill and Gus's puppy—a hint that perhaps Gus and Jill were childless. Because of Jill's frigidity? Because Gus wanted children and she did not? A flash tale often leaves some things unanswered, or answerable in more ways than one.

The last several sentences seal up the ambiguity: Gus kisses Jill on the cheek, but she doesn't respond. He goes into the kitchen for a drink; Cheri walks in *after a decent interval*, looking ill. (Note the ironic counterpoint of "decent" with the *in*decency of their affair.) The last sentence, "I could see what she was thinking," resonates ironically with Rod's comment about Cheri's face being a sufficient vehicle for confession. Also Gus had become attuned to the subtleties of Cheri's expressions to have so quickly discerned her thoughts.

Purpose: Aesop always tagged on an explicit moral to each of his fables, making these stories ideal for young people to connect the story situations to real-life purpose. Adults, though, do not need to be told the explicit purpose or moral of the story; it spoils the fun of individual reflection. The purpose or moral of "The Confession" should be obvious anyway: Being unfaithful to one's spouse can have terrible consequences.

Now you might wonder, did I plan all these nuances beforehand? No. My advice is trust your creative intuition to do much of this work for you. The story was conceived as a question: What if a guy had an affair with his close friend's wife? The next questions that popped into my head as I began the story were, "What if this guy's friend harbors violent, even murderous tendencies? What if his wife is scared to death of him for that reason?" The point here is that once you get the germ of a story, once you start working on the story in earnest, the nuances will fall into place.

Analysis of a Genre Flash Story

The differences between "literary" and "genre" fiction are not as clear-cut in flash fiction as they are in novels. Thriller or mystery fans looking for the latest Greg Iles or Sara Paretsky novel to take to the beach expect a story with a page-turning plot and strong characters grappling with harrowing situations. Whereas in literary fiction the emphasis is on theme and complexities of character, in genre fiction the emphasis is on plot, on what is going to happen. Try conducting your own analysis of my science fiction tale that follows:

A Community Reckoning

by Fred D. White

Two of the judges came for the teacher at high noon. They brought her to the central plaza in the community where a wooden stage had been cobbled together alongside a white-marble statue of one of the founders raising his arms to Heaven. An outsider might have mistaken it for a gallows platform; but all that had been placed on it was a folding chair.

One of the judges clipped a microphone to his white robe. "Sit," he ordered the teacher as if addressing a dog. Like a magician about to perform a trick, the other judge proffered a spool of red ribbon to the audience. He then unwound a yard or so of the ribbon, snipped it with comically oversized scissors, and secured the teacher to the chair with it as the teacher glared at him. He unspooled more ribbon, snipped it, and bound her feet. The judge then cut a third strip of ribbon to gently bind her slender wrists. "We don't want your discomfort to interfere with your concentration." Finally, he gagged her and then asked her to say something.

"Urrmph!" she said.

The judge nodded approvingly to the other judge.

Now that the teacher was secured, a strikingly tall man wearing a star-spangled top hat and striped pants and carrying a velvet pouch mounted the stage. He nodded to the judges, then faced the audience and bowed to applause; and after everyone quieted, he turned severely to the teacher. "You, teacher, have been destabilizing our blessed community with your propaganda."

"Urrmpph!" She shook her head fiercely.

"Oh yes," he continued. "Gone are the days when you so-called educators decide on the kinds of knowledge to teach, or how to teach it—especially alleged scientific knowledge."

The teacher continued shaking her head and uttering "Urrmph!"—those being the only ways she was able to communicate. Tall Man watched her struggle against her ribbon constraints for a moment; then he continued: "You have broken your pledge never to undercut our students' peace with the community, and with their beloved parents."

The teacher emitted an anguished sound through her gag.

Tall Man leaned toward the teacher, mockingly cupping his ear. "Eh? Eh? Is that a new word you've added to your already bloated vocabulary?"

That brought scattered laughter from the crowd.

Tall Man turned to face the audience. With a flourish, he doffed his top hat, releasing a cascade of blond hair. The audience cheered, and Tall Man replaced his hat and broke into a little jig. A woman in the crowd yelled, "Let's get the show on the road!"—which was followed by other voices: "Amen to that!" "Bring out the student!" Tall Man extended the palms of his hands. "We must not be hasty." Once the shouting died away, he retrieved the velvet pouch, held it up, spread it open, and pulled out a golden handled filleting knife, which he proffered to the audience as if it were a holy relic. There were cheers, intermixed with gasps of awe. The teacher uttered a new guttural sound through her gag.

Tall Man looked over his shoulder at the woman. "This has a way of concentrating the mind, does it not, Miz Smarter than the Rest of Us?" He held up the knife in a way that allowed it to catch the sun's reflection. "The teacher may have conveyed her alleged evidence about the nature of physical reality to our precious youth with the best of intentions," he said to the crowd. "That is to say, she may have convinced herself that mathematical truths, and microscopic or *fossilized* truths"—that last phrase triggered a few bubbles of laughter—"supersede *the* Truth, capital T, unaware of the irreversible damage she was causing her students." He paused as if to relish the now rapt attentiveness of the audience. "But our teacher here grossly underestimated her students' capacity for—" he was interrupted by a new volley of cheering "—for her students' readiness to defy their teacher's fake truths at all costs."

Two judges now brought onto the stage a fifteen- or sixteen-year-old girl wearing a black skirt, black scarf, and open-collared black blouse. She curtsied before Tall Man and positioned herself directly in front of the teacher.

Dead silence.

And then: "You've ruined my mind, teacher!" shrieked the student as she accepted the filleting knife from Tall Man. "I will tell you the unforgivable sin I committed in my loving home yesterday!"

The teacher bowed her head, shaking it slowly—possibly her pathetic effort to negate the student's testimony.

"Yesterday I told my loving father and mother that they were IGNORANT!" And with a grand sweep of her arm, she slashed the knife across her own neck—seeing to it, as she'd been instructed, that her blood sprayed directly into the teacher's horrified face before she collapsed at the gagged woman's ribbon-bound feet.

—first published in *The Hungry Chimera* 4; Feb. 2018. Web.

Analysis

Story-ness: The genre I'm working in here is dystopian science fiction, a subgenre made famous by George Orwell in *Nineteen Eighty-Four*, Ray Bradbury in *Fahrenheit 451*, Philip K. Dick in *Do Androids Dream of Electric Sheep?* (Ridley Scott adapted it for the screen as *Blade Runner*), and Shirley Jackson in her short story "The Lottery." The world I've conjured up is one in which dissent from parental authority carries a severe penalty—ironically less for the primary dissenter (the teacher) than for the secondary one (the student). From the very first sentence, I aimed to generate keen curiosity: What kind of society is this? What is going on here? And then, after the first two paragraphs, What is going to happen next? These are the questions that should arise from a genre story.

Immediate engagement: The opening sentence sets the scene, introduces the situation, and (I hope) causes the reader to wonder, what the hell is going on here?

Distinctive narrative voice: I wanted the narrator to come across as a disinterested observer or reporter. That way, the grimness—the dystopian horror—of the situation would come through more forcefully.

Authentic characters: This was a tricky criterion for me to meet: how do I make these characters seem real and weird at the same time? I realized that I could actually enhance Tall Man's weirdness by giving him identifiable attributes, such as vanity and vindictiveness.

Purpose: "A Community Reckoning" is dramatic hyperbole, an extreme example of what could happen to public education if a community mandated parental authority, coupled with blind patriotism, to be non-negotiable.

Analysis of a Humorous Flash Story

There are a great many different kinds of humorous tales, though they all share something in common: they are a delight to read. Humor is not necessarily synonymous with gags, but humorous tales are all light-hearted. Flash humor has the terseness of a good joke, but it isn't a joke (although jokes can be embedded in them)—which is to say, it does not depend on a punch line. Let's take a look at a flash humor piece and then see what makes it work.

Double Date

by Peter Cherches

It's a Shakespearean double date—Hamlet and Ophelia and Macbeth and Lady Macbeth go to a restaurant, a steak house. It turns into a comedy of errors. As soon as they arrive, Lady Macbeth heads to the ladies' room to wash her hands, and she stays in there for twenty minutes. And Ophelia's such a weirdo—in the middle of a conversation she starts singing snatches of old songs. Then, every time the waiter comes to take their order, Hamlet says he needs a few more minutes to decide. When they're finally ready to order, it turns out that Hamlet and Ophelia don't even want steak—Ophelia orders the California Platter and Hamlet says, "I'll just have a Danish." The Macbeths are big meat eaters, though, and they both ask for the 16-ounce New York cut. Macbeth orders his medium rare but Lady Macbeth wants hers well done—the sight of blood nauseates her. While they're waiting for the food to come the Macbeths try to make small talk, but it's a losing proposition—Hamlet is sullen and morose and Ophelia's in her own world. When the food finally arrives there's another problem—both steaks are well done.

"Call the waiter," Lady Macbeth says. "Tell him to take it back."

"That's all right, dear," Macbeth says. "I'll eat this one."

"You ordered medium rare!"

"Yes, but I don't want to make a scene."

"Don't be such a wimp," Lady Macbeth says. "Send it back!"

"All right, dear," Macbeth says, and motions for the waiter.

When the waiter gets to their table, he insists that both Macbeths ordered their steaks well done.

"Are you going to take that from this prick?" Lady Macbeth screeches.

"No, dear," Macbeth replies, and kills the waiter.

Hamlet, who has just taken the first bite of his Danish, spits it out all over the table. "Yecch," he says. "Something's rotten."

On top of everything else, the Macbeths drink so much coffee that they might as well kiss the idea of sleep good night.

—first published in *North American Review*; reprinted in *Flash Fiction Funny*, ed. Tom Hazuka; Blue Light Press 2013

Analysis

Story-ness: "Double-Date" is an example of mash-up fiction: incidents and characters from different times, places, or (in this case) literary sources coming together in a way that makes us laugh. So here we have indecisive Hamlet and emotionally unstable Ophelia double dating with bloodthirsty, avaricious Macbeth and his aggressive wife Lady Macbeth in a modern-day restaurant and having a run-in with their waiter.

Immediate engagement: "Double Date" is a clever example of literary humor; readers need to be familiar with Hamlet and Macbeth to appreciate the witticisms to the fullest—which is a safe bet because most readers would have read these plays in high school. Notice how the author sets the stage in the very first sentence. And in the second sentence—"It is a comedy of errors"—promises further comic references to follow.

Distinctive narrative voice: The narrator's jocular tone is sustained and buttressed by the numerous comic parallels between the events in the restaurant and their serious counterparts in Shakespeare's plays, such as Lady Macbeth spending twenty minutes in the ladies room washing her hands.

Authentic characters: Okay, "authentic" may be a stretch in the context of humorous flash, but the author has certainly been consistent in extending the temperaments of these Shakespearean characters.

Purpose: By placing two of Shakespeare's best known serious characters into a modern-day casual context—yet still retaining something of their original natures—the author not only evokes laughter, but shows how memorable, three-dimensional characters transcend the era in which they were conceived.

Analysis of an Experimental Flash Story

"Experimental" carries a lot of conflicting connotations. Let's sort them out. The term, as it is typically used by editors, refers to stories that do not adhere to typical narrative structure, but may include elements associated with poetry or nonfiction, or the visual arts. It does not mean an arbitrary tossing into the story of whatever comes to mind—experimentation for its own sake.

I've always been fascinated by those enigmatic Zen *koans* (which, come to think of it, have much in common with flash fiction!). One day, while stopping for lunch at a Jewish deli, I started thinking of the similarity between the word *koan* and the name Cohen. At the same time I was watching an employee behind the counter slicing some corned beef for a customer. *Shazam!* My flash fiction goddess-muse sent me the germ of what eventually became the following story:

Uncle Hilbert's *Cohens*
by Fred D. White

A rabbi walks into a delicatessen, asks for two pounds of corned beef, very lean, lots of fat. Moishe, the counterman, nods. "Certainly, Rabbi." He grabs a brisket, heads to the slicer and freezes. "Excuse me, Rabbi. Did you say lean or fat?" "Lean!" the Rabbi shouts. "Fat!" Moishe stares slack-jawed at his esteemed customer. Then he grabs a second brisket, proffers them both. "Here is lean. Here is fat. Tell me what you want." The rabbi raises his hands to heaven and wails. In a flash Moishe realizes what the rabbi wants.

Uncle Hilbert Cohen served his grandnephew his pastrami sandwich and waited for him to respond.

"It's a paradox," ventured Davy, "just like that Zen *koan* about one hand clapping." He bit into his sandwich.

"Not a paradox. My *Cohens* are nothing like those absurd Zen *koans*."

"Either the rabbi wants lean or he wants fat. To want both is contradictory."

"Not contradictory. Did Moishe not hold up two briskets? Can you not slice from both for one customer? Can you not love both lean and fat? You must learn to think like a *person*, not like a machine."

"Well, it seems to me that the rabbi could have made his request clearer."

"No, the rabbi made his request perfectly clear. He wanted Moishe to realize that corned beef tastes best when you do not separate in your mind lean from fat—that, in the mind of God, there are no paradoxes. Can you understand that?" His uncle excused himself to wait on a customer.

When he returned, Davy raised his hands to heaven—suddenly realizing with embarrassment that he made the same gesture as the rabbi in the *Cohen*. "I'm sorry, Uncle, I simply do not have a head for your *Cohens*."

Uncle Hilbert sat down and gazed sadly at Davy.

"Please don't be disappointed in me, Uncle. So I'm not good at Talmudic reasoning; but I have other qualities."

"Talmudic reasoning, as you call it, is of fundamental importance to life. You must learn to pay attention."

"I was paying attention."

"Not close enough."

Davy sighed. "Okay. I'll listen more carefully for the clues."

"No; you will pay *close attention*." Uncle Hilbert wagged a finger. "My *Cohens* are occasions for careful thinking; they're not parlor games."

Davy nodded solemnly.

"Now listen—*pay attention*—to this next *Cohen*."

Davy folded his hands, shut his eyes, and listened.

Mel and Gus are camping in the Sierras. They rejoice in the crisp, fresh air, the Ponderosa pines, the majestic waterfalls and snow-capped peaks. "We spend far too much time in the city," Mel says, breathing deeply. Gus replies, "In this place I feel inside out. I must return at once to the city."

Davy opened his eyes. "Gus rejects the natural world, majestic as it is, as a substitute for the inner peace he feels when he's in the chaotic city. It is better to locate the beauty and tranquility of nature *within* oneself."

Uncle Hilbert pressed his lips together. "Not bad for leaping without looking. But you must not leap with my *Cohens*. Do you want to think further about Gus's response?"

Davy realized what he had overlooked. "Inner, outer . . . To separate the two is to be cut off from both?"

That earned Davy a smile from his uncle. "You're catching on."

"So do you think I'll qualify for rabbinical school after all?

"Maybe, maybe not. I have one more *Cohen* for you"

It is June, 1945. Hilbert returns from the charnel house that the war has made of Europe and goes straight to the apartment of his fiancée, Sasha, wondering if she will keep her promise to marry him if he survived, no matter what toll the war took on him. Sasha opens the door and gasps. "Is it really you?" "What is left of me," Hilbert replies. She stares into his eyes. "Oh no, oh no," she manages to say and shuts the door in his face.

"And then what?" said Davy.

"That's it. That's my whole *Cohen*," said Uncle Hilbert.

Davy shook his head. "I'm not yet ready for rabbinical school."

"You neglected to pay attention, to think with your *soul*."

"Maybe I don't have a soul."

"You have a soul. You just need to connect it to your brain."

"Very well, let me try again. Please repeat the *Cohen* to me."

Uncle Hilbert complied.

Davy cogitated as deeply as he could for several minutes. Finally, he spoke carefully: "You survived for two years in the Valley of Death; but . . . ."

"'But' . . .?"

"But even though you were able to leave the Valley of Death, it never left you."

"And what does that have to do with Sasha rejecting me?"

"I'm thinking! Did a part of you die after all?"

"Why are you asking? You are supposed to be interpreting, not asking."

Davy suppressed a groan. "When Sasha looked into your eyes, she saw the part of you that had died . . ."

"Go on, go on."

"Unfortunately, the part of you that had died was the part that made it possible for you to love. And—and even though you already knew that, you had to let Sasha see it for herself."

Uncle Hilbert rubbed his chin. "You are beginning to show promise."

"*Beginning?* What am I overlooking?"

"What indeed." Uncle Hilbert ran a hand through his disheveled white hair. "What you are overlooking, what we who have survived are overlooking, is the greater death that has infiltrated our collective hearts."

—first published in *Atticus Review*, Feb. 2015. Web.

Analysis

Creative thinking comes when you allow disparate thoughts and impressions to swirl around in your brain. It's a prerequisite for avant-garde writing. As I began working with the idea of an elderly Jewish World War Two veteran (Hilbert Cohen) conjuring up his own brand of Zen *koans* ("Cohens"), it eventually struck me that this could become a series of linked morality tales, culminating in one of devastating loss—yet all the while serving to impart important moral lessons to Hilbert's nephew, Davy.

Story-ness: This is a story in which three stories ("Cohens") are told, each one shedding light on Hilbert's moral outlook (the prime story). The third Cohen serves as a kind of dark window into the root of Uncle Hilbert's unhappy life.

Immediate engagement: I attempted to hook the reader by opening with the first of Hilbert's "Cohens"—an anecdote that is both funny and wise.

Distinctive narrative voice: Hilbert as narrator of the "Cohens" comes across as rabbinical, a moral teacher who wants to impart wisdom to his grand-nephew.

Authentic characters: In a virtually all-dialogue story such as this, one must make sure that the dialogue captures the characters' respective personalities. Does Hilbert emerge as the wise old man whose wisdom was gained partly by misfortune, who hopes that he can at least impart necessary wisdom to a younger generation, represented by his grand-nephew? Does Davy come across at first as somewhat naïve, and in the course of the story, grows a bit wiser as a result of paying attention to his great uncle's stories? Those were my intentions.

Purpose: Ancient teachings that grapple with complex moral issues (typified by ancient Zen *koans*) have a counterpart in the modern world.

Now It's Time to Pick Up Your Pen

A note on the goal of these exercises: In addition to stimulating your creative storytelling imagination, the selection of exercises below are designed to heighten your powers of analysis. As this chapter has tried to show, the ability to analyze fiction is as important as the ability to compose it.

1. Imagine a dystopian society in which all sexual deviance has been outlawed. First write a description of this stricture. How does this society define sexual deviance? Does it tolerate any gray areas? What are the penalties?
    a. In a single sentence, write the premise of the story.
    b. Expand the story into a one-paragraph synopsis.
    c. (optional) Write a profile for each of the principal characters.
    d. Draft the story.
    e. Read it aloud to catch overlooked gaps in continuity or awkward sentences.
    f. Reread your story with a critical eye, and revise.
2. Make a list of word- or name-pairs that sound the same but are different. Next, choose one pair and conjure up a flash tale premise around it. Example: Indian (Native American) and Indian (one who is from or resides in India). Story premise: Two college roommates, a Native American and an Asian Indian, discover ways to use their

knowledge of their respective ancestors' mistreatment (by Western settlers; by British colonial rule) to help solve their conflicts with other students and with their own inward struggles. Other pairings that could generate story ideas: entrance (to a room) / entrance (mesmerize); club (organization) / club (cudgel).

3. Take out one of your old stories and, using the criteria discussed in this chapter, write a complete analysis of the story.
4. Write an all-dialogue flash tale in which two people are arguing over how best to analyze a particular work of art. Possible art objects:
   - A Picasso painting, such as *Guernica*
   - An abstract expressionist painting (e.g., one of Jackson Pollack's "drip" paintings)
   - Andrew Wyeth's *Christina's World*
   - Grant Wood's *American Gothic*
   - Any modernist work of art of your choice
5. Write an analysis of the following flash tale by yours truly, using the criteria for analysis discussed in this chapter.

The Great Camilla
by Fred D. White

> If this be magic, let it be an art
> Lawful as eating.
> —Shakespeare, *The Winter's Tale*, V.iii

The Great Camilla drifted out of her dream, sad not to have experienced the bliss of being neither here nor there a while longer. Even a mage like her needed a respite from all the shape-changing she was expected to perform.

At least she had discovered a universe in which magic was both a reality and a rarity, not just a bag of tricks. She took pleasure in astonishing audiences with her feats of transformation and displacement. Of course, if they knew beforehand that she was a true mage, not an illusionist, she would be feared instead of admired, perhaps even arrested. So the Great Camilla restricted her magic to simple yet amazing transformations like changing a goldfish into an angelfish or turning a scarf into a snake. She refrained from the bizarre. Once, she foolishly imbued a month-old infant with the ability to speak ("I will grow up to be a magician like the Great Camilla!" warbled the infant in its mother's ear). The mother shrieked and dropped the infant, causing the babe to yell, "*What the fuck?!*"

"Simple ventriloquism," explained the Great Camilla during an interrogation. Anyone can learn to do it; it shouldn't even qualify as an illusion, let alone sorcery."

"Except that my baby spoke those words in my *ear*," the rattled mother insisted.

"And I heard her holler, '*What the f-word*.'"

"So what do you propose to do?" Camilla asked the mother's attorney. "Have me arrested on suspicion of extreme ventriloquism?"

"We'd like you to tell us more about your, uhm, act."

"You want to know how I perform my tricks, in other words. Would you have interrogated Harry Houdini on similar suspicions?"

"Harry *who?*"

"Never mind." She had forgotten which universe she'd wound up in.

"Look, Camilla, you can make this a lot easier on yourself if you'll just cooperate."

And so the Great Camilla was compelled to use even more of her genuine magic to keep herself out of the slammer—not that a jail cell could have held her, not even in this dreary universe where Harry Houdini never existed. She snapped her fingers, and the judge, attorney, and child's mother turned into little plastic game toys.

If only . . .

If only she hadn't tinkered with reality-shifting. But that was the price she had to pay for allowing her wizardry to overrule her judgment. The greatest feat of magic she could accomplish would be to rematerialize into Houdini's universe, assuming she could find it again, a universe in which magicians were no more than illusionists (although Houdini had been more than an illusionist). There she would be admired rather than scorned or feared. She might even engage in some major reality transformations: she'd heard about the atrocities committed in that reality—atrocities she could disrupt if not prevent with her magic—and no one would ever accuse her of sorcery.

—first published in *Mad Hat Lit.*, Nov. 2014. Web.

Part Two

The Nuts and Bolts of Writing Flash

4

Writing Genre Flash Fiction

If you are new to flash fiction, I suggest you practice writing genre flash stories before other kinds. It is important for fiction writers of any stripe to be able to tell a well-made story. As you write a genre flash story, you are focusing keenly on structure: establishing the conflict situation, working in one or more complications, and figuring out how to pace the story effectively, while at the same time depicting your characters and the setting vividly and realistically. Even the non-genre-specific variants (literary stories, humor/satire, or experimental types) are essentially stories that present, at least implicitly, one or more characters struggling against someone or something, and who, as a result of the struggle, achieve some result or experience some epiphany, for good or ill. Of course, that foundation of story-ness can be rendered in different ways. For example, a story can open *in medias res*—in the middle of a situation (ideal for hooking the reader) before the situation is clarified through the use of back-story information or flashbacks; or the story can open where it would customarily end, with flashbacks gradually piecing the puzzle together.

In a novel, numerous dramatic moments are rendered in detail. In genre flash fiction, however, there is room for only a single such moment or a string of closely interconnected moments to be so rendered.

How Traditional Story Structure Works in Flash Fiction

Let's take a closer look at how traditional plot structure (situation-complication-climax-conclusion) construction works in extremely brief tales—even in the briefest, the six-word story (yes, this is a bona fide sub-genre of flash fiction), like this one, famously attributed to Ernest Hemingway:

For sale:
baby shoes.
Never worn.

The first two words comprise the situation. We don't know what is for sale yet, or why, but our curiosity is instantly aroused. The subsequent two words do two things: they tell us what is for sale, but then they also instantly raise the key question: Why would anyone offer *baby shoes* for sale? In just two words, a complication has been established. Then come the last two gut-wrenching words that comprise the climax/resolution. The resolution is actually inconclusive because the reader must provide the most logical implication of "never worn": not that the baby shoes were the wrong size, not that they were an unattractive style or color, not that the parents were unsentimental, but that the baby did not survive.

Virtually all fiction, especially genre fiction, relies on this fundamental structure. For flash fiction writers, the challenge increases in difficulty because there is so little room to work up convincing and engaging content around that framework. But if Hemingway (assuming he actually did write "Baby Shoes") could do it in six words, the rest of us can do it in a thousand or fewer.

Before we move on to more detailed step-by-step guidelines for writing genre flash tales, let me dwell a bit longer on six-word stories. Practicing writing them makes for excellent concision training. I once began drafting a story that I hoped would convey the tragedy of preventable killings of African Americans by police. I'd written page after page of confrontation between police officers and a black driver whom the officers pulled over because, let's say, of a burnt-out tail light. The man panics and the panic is misinterpreted as insubordination, which escalates into apparent resisting arrest, and so on. But after several pages, I still hadn't conveyed the impact I wanted. And then in a flash of insight, I turned those seven pages into six words, plus a title:

Black Lives Matter
by Fred D. White

"Hands up!"
He obeyed.
They fired.

In flash fiction, less is more. Sometimes a great deal more. The reversal of expectation, the shocking absence of anything resembling human compassion conveyed by the last two words of my "Black Lives Matter," may not correspond to what had actually occurred in 2014 in Ferguson, Missouri, or elsewhere; rather, it uses hyperbole (exaggeration, a device common to humor and satire; see Chapter 6) to call attention to the fact that some (very few) police officers lack sufficient compassion for human life when the human being in question is a person of color.

Crafting a Genre Flash Story

Let's get down to the business of crafting a flash story with a plot. Below, you will find a list of seven steps which will guide you through the story-crafting process. Keep in mind that the steps I lay out below can be modified to suit your temperament. For example, if you are uncomfortable adhering to *any* kind of step-by-step procedure, then go ahead and plunge into a draft and see where it takes you. It might take you down a dead-end street, in which case you will try drafting something different. Trial-and-error suits some writers just fine. The problem is that it's labor intensive, time consuming, and rather frustrating. Following a procedure like the seven steps that follow will help you become more efficient, more productive.

These are the seven steps:

1. Brainstorm
2. Capture the gist of the story in a single sentence
3. Expand the sentence into a one-paragraph synopsis
4. Draft the story
5. Take a break
6. Read the story aloud
7. Revise the story.

Step One: Brainstorm

As I noted in Chapter 1, this should be the first step for any kind of flash fiction—indeed, for fiction of any length. The reason is that so much of what you know is tacit—in other words just out of reach of your consciousness—and only comes into consciousness when you prod it, which is what brainstorming does.

You might have expected Step One to be "Choose the genre," but no. It's best not to think of genre at all unless you're already an established writer of science fiction or fantasy or mystery and are adept at writing for a specific market. By brainstorming first, you're aiming to conjure up an intriguing character faced with some kind of predicament, and who must find a way to resolve the predicament despite one or more daunting obstacles, including psychological ones. In a flash tale, these elements must be laid out quickly and with great concision. Conventional short story elements such as setting and back story and multiple confrontations can only be hinted at.

Brainstorming should proceed rapidly, with your internal editor switched off; otherwise, it will be self-defeating. The purpose is to generate possible material, not to compose an actual story. I prefer to brainstorm with pen and paper, away from my desk. A lounge chair will do nicely, especially if there's a nice cool beverage on the table next to you.

Step Two: Capture the gist of the story in a single sentence

Imagine someone asking you, "What is the story about?" You should be able to state its essence in one sentence, and a simple sentence at that. But writing that simple sentence in a way that accurately captures what you want the story to accomplish is challenging. Expect to write several drafts of the sentence before you are satisfied with it.

Let's look at a couple examples. First, if someone were to ask me, in regard to my flash story "The Confession" (which appears in Chapter 3), "What is that story about?" I would answer, "It is about the harrowing predicament someone falls into when he has an affair with his best friend's wife." As for the science fiction flash story of mine, "Brainies," which appears below, I would say, "It is about a young career person—ambitious but seriously lacking in self-confidence—who wishes to purchase an ingenious new invention to give him the knowledge and confidence he needs, but cannot afford it."

Step Three: Expand the sentence into a one-paragraph synopsis

It's important to have a strong sense of not only what your story is about, but also of how the story unfolds (obstacles blocking the desired outcome and what the protagonist does to overcome them), and the underlying theme you want the story to convey. A one-paragraph synopsis includes these story elements. If you're having a difficult time writing the synopsis, chances are you do not yet have a firm grip on your story. If that is the case, do some more brainstorming.

You're probably wondering, if a flash story is already highly condensed, why bother with a synopsis at all? Well, there are two kinds of condensation. A good flash story may be highly condensed, but it is not a summary or a stripped-down-to-bare-essence version of what should really be a longer story. The synopsis, however, *is* stripped down and summative. Put into a synopsis whatever is necessary for anyone to understand the story in its essence. The synopsis puts you on the story-drafting track. Once you have a synopsis, all that's needed for drafting is to delineate (render dramatically) the key elements.

One day, I decided to write a flash science fiction story set in a future in which one can purchase undergarments with nanobots (microscopic robots) woven into the fabric that instantly connect with the wearer's brain to make him or her expert in a particular field (which, by the way, was my premise sentence). This is how I extended that premise for my synopsis:

> Gregg Byrd has an opportunity to become a star public relations person with a flying automobile dealership. However he faces two obstacles: he has difficulty speaking assertively and persuasively to groups, and he can't afford to purchase the "Pitch Master" Brainie—the undergarment containing nanobots that would turn him into a top-notch salesman. However, as soon as he dons the Brainie to test it out, he uses his sudden surge of PR skill to try and persuade Cynthia the saleslady to look the other way while he absconds with the garment. Alas, his scheme fails because . . . (I won't give away the ending so you can enjoy the story, reproduced below.)

Step Four: Draft the story

My advice here (based on my own writing habits) is to dive into the draft, almost like you're brainstorming—except that you know the premise of your story and understand the genre framework. What I'm saying is write rapidly without worrying about stylistic or grammatical matters; if you do, it impedes your narrative progression, your *storytelling*. Stylistic refinements are for the revision stage.

Step Five: Take a break

It is important to acquire critical distance from the draft you've just completed. In my own experience, this can vary from one day to a week or more. Psychologists who study creativity will tell you that an "incubation" period is a vital stage in any artistic production. That's because the subconscious mind needs time to let things percolate. Incubate? Percolate? I'm probably mixing metaphors, but you get the picture. Oh—and by "take a break" I mean from the story, not from writing. Get busy on another story.

Step Six: Read the story aloud

I suspect you don't encounter this step very often. Read aloud? To whom? And why?

Very often, you will catch awkward syntax or gaps in story progression when you read the story aloud. Genre flash fiction tends to require the maximum length limit (1000 words) or close to it in order to work convincingly as a plotted story. Even so, plot progression and coherence can be tricky in so limited a space. Reading aloud is a good way to test those story elements.

Step Seven: Revise, revise!

One of my favorite mottoes is "Writing is Rewriting." I have written more than a hundred flash stories, and not once did any of them come out right the first time. Some I've revised several times before I could finally assure myself that it was as good as I could make it. Also, quite frankly, some of my stories didn't pass muster even after several revisions.

But 90 percent of the time, I have made flawed tales publishable through careful revision. The trick is to make sure you're sufficiently distanced from the story so you can anatomize it with a cold, critical eye. Sure, let others read and comment on the draft (if you trust their critical acumen), but ultimately you must become your own harshest critic.

When it comes to revising a flash tale, sometimes the best approach is to rewrite it in its entirety. This is what is called substantive revision: you're revising to reshape the story itself, to strengthen the plot, make the characters seem more authentic, and the setting more evocative.

I cannot over-emphasize the importance of substantive revision, whether you're an old pro or a neophyte. Sometimes that means reassessing your statement of what the story is about, or even tossing the existing draft in the circular file and beginning anew, or "revising from spirit," as F. Scott Fitzgerald advised.

A second type of revision is stylistic: First of all, is the story *readable*? Clunky or verbose sentences can disrupt readability. An imprecise word, even a grammatical error, can throw a reader out of the story.

Anatomy of a Genre Flash Story

Let's look closely at (by which I mean take apart) the science fiction flash that I introduced above. I choose this one because not only is it plotted, but it is also unconventional, and in two ways. One, the narrator is something of an anti-hero, a loser; and two, the story is humorous, humor generally being a separate category (see Chapter 6). However, I really do want to reinforce the point that different types of flash fiction can be intermingled.

Brainies

by Fred D. White

"We like to think of them as new-life undergarments, Mr. Byrd," Cynthia the saleswoman proclaimed as she held up one of the latest Brainies (a Chess Master Brainie) by the sleeves, "for the simple reason that they can change your life dramatically."

Gregg Byrd ran his hands over the silky fabric. There was no way to guess, just from sight or touch, that the glittery blue undergarment contained a layer of nanobots that, once activated (via purchase), assimilate themselves inside the owner's brain.

"I invite you to sample one," Cynthia said. "Choose a skill you dream of mastering; chances are, we stock a Brainie for it. A temporary activation code will enable you to experience ten minutes of enhanced knowledge and/or motor skill in an area of your choice." She must have noticed Gregg's confusion, for she quickly added, "Of course, the trial bots will self-destruct after the trial period, with no adverse effects on your brain cells."

Gregg took the Tablet she handed him and scrolled through the long list. "I'm, like, hoping to, you know, land a job in, uh, marketing," he muttered half to himself.

"Ah, then perhaps you are looking for a Pitch Master Brainie."

"Uh, yeah, sure—that sounds about right."

She pointed at the Tablet. "Go ahead, tell it what you want."

Gregg cleared his throat and said, "I, uh—" He cleared his throat again and took a deep breath. "Uh, er. . . I would like the P-Pitch Master, uh, option."

"Please restate your request."

"Don't use unnecessary words like 'option'—that'll only confuse it. Also, avoid saying 'uh' or 'er' and try not to stammer."

"Pitch Master!" Gregg bleated.

"One Pitch Master remaining, extra large."

"It's, like, a size too large for me, Cynthia, b-but I'll try it on anyway, if that's okay."

She smiled serenely. "I strongly recommend that."

He doubted that ten minutes would be enough time for the Brainie to convince him that it could transform him from a stutterer with stage fright to a masterful public speaker, aglow with confidence, capable of enrapturing prospective clients— but that was what he dreamed of becoming, and there was nothing to lose by trying it on. It would be an extremely expensive purchase, of course. Rentals, once permitted, were suspended after a rash of illegal nanobot replications.

Cynthia led him to a room where she waited for him to remove his shirt and don the Brainie. "I must lock you in for the trial. As you can well imagine, these garments are popular with thieves."

"I bet."

She entered the trial activation code on her Tablet. "Also, this particular Brainie requires me to remain in the room with you—as your audience."

Gregg smiled. Something delightful began stirring in his head. "That would give me the greatest pleasure!" He spread his arms wide, as if to embrace her.

Cynthia showed no reaction. Some women, he thought, required more savoir faire before they could be charmed. Well, just give him another few minutes . . .

"I'm ready for your pitch, Mr. Byrd."

"Call me Gregg." He cleared his throat. "Now then: As a prospective writer of a ten-million dollar advertising campaign for Mercedes-Air, I will be scripting irresistible scenarios of young people enthralled by the experience of piloting their own Mercedes Airmobile over the city, over gridlocked freeways and decaying bridges, over treacherous mountain roads, literally on top of the world! And furthermore . . ." Gregg was mesmerized by the steady stream of eloquent words rushing from his mouth—and more than that, a vigorous and seductive delivery of those eloquent words that captured the pleasures of air-mobile performance, the unforgettable thrill of maneuvering a 6874-SL-wingjet—

Cynthia sat, hands folded, mouth partly open. Were her eyes dilated? Why, yes! The Pitch Master was working splendidly.

An electronic voice crackled. *Five minutes remaining.*

A fiendish thought wriggled its way into Gregg Byrd's head. In a voice more fulsome and caressing than he could ever have dreamed of possessing, he told Cynthia he'd been waiting his whole life to meet a woman as radiant as she, a woman to whom he would joyously devote his life, if only she would enter the code for the purchase transaction, and simply look the other way as he absconded with the Pitch Master Brainie.

Cynthia shuddered as if snapping out of a trance. She leaped to her feet and grabbed him in a choke-hold. "Those of us who sell Brainies are required to wear a Brainie as well. Did you know that, Mr. Byrd?" she hissed in his ear.

Gregg could only gasp for air.

Ping. The sound came from the Brainie tag: His ten-minute trial period was over.

Cynthia slammed him against the wall. "Well? Did you?"

"Uh . . . N-no!"

"It's called a Store Detective Brainie." And with lightning speed, she cuffed him and instructed her Tablet to summon the police.

—first published in *Every Day Fiction*, May, 2017. Web.

An aside: I originally titled this story "Smarties," but changed it after an editor reminded me that "Smarties" was a brand of candy, and that the association might clash with my intentions. She was right. Titles are important—after all, they're the first words read, and offer a hint as to what follows.

How did I come up with this idea? It's a tricky question, because I have to probe my subconscious mind for part of the answer. For years I've wondered about how people could become smarter using artificial means—implants, say, or teaching machines that educate you while you're asleep, or brain surgery that can raise your IQ, as in Daniel Keyes's classic novel, *Flowers for Algernon* (made into the movie *Charly*). Also, there's a tinge of autobiography in this little yarn: Even after nearly forty years of classroom teaching and giving dozens of presentations at academic conferences, I've never been at ease speaking to an audience. The only thing that kept me from being a total nervous wreck was to over-prepare.

To make a genre flash story work, you have to make sure you have a story, a situation in which the protagonist engages in some kind of struggle to get what he or she wants: a material goal, an immaterial goal (like freedom to do something or freedom from something), or maybe, as in "Brainies," a primary goal (to be an expert speaker/public relations person) and secondary goal (to obtain the Brainie that would ensure that primary goal). There may even be a tertiary goal: the affection (or at least the aiding and abetting) of the saleslady.

As in all kinds of genre fiction, the goal(s) cannot come easily. Struggle, compounded by setback, is the essence of story-ness. Poor Gregg Byrd desperately needs the Pitch Master Brainie, but can't afford it. His desperation leads him to woo Cynthia with his newly acquired (but temporary) persuasive powers. Alas, the scheme backfires, as Cynthia, all too aware of how popular Brainies are with thieves, must wear a Store Detective Brainie to deal with the problem.

How should one go about plotting a genre flash tale? In this particular case I wrote a draft once I got the germ of the idea about an undergarment that could make people smarter, and just kept rewriting until I had something that worked. I follow the seven-step procedure I've outlined above; but with "Brainies" I did a couple of the steps out of order, or more than once. For example, I brainstormed a second time after I scribbled out a not-so-convincing synopsis; then I rewrote the synopsis after I wrote a first draft.

Now It's Time to Pick Up Your Pen

1. Brainstorm for a genre flash tale—say a romance—drawing from personal experience. But change things around so that you're not writing part of an autobiography. First come up with a situation, the more unusual the better—for example, a female lifeguard falls in love with a scuba diver as she struggles to save his life after he'd been bitten by a shark. Whatever the situation, depict it in as much vivid detail as you can. Authenticity matters in flash fiction, just as it does in novels.
2. Get to work on a flash tale that combines two genres, such as romance and fantasy, science fiction and mystery, romance and horror, mystery and humor, and so on.
    a. Start by brainstorming for a one-sentence story premise
    b. Turn the premise into a one-paragraph synopsis
    c. Draft the story
    d. Set the draft aside for one or two days
    e. Read the story aloud
    f. Revise the story
3. Choose one or more of the following story premises and follow steps b–f above.
    - A woman hires a private detective to search for her lost husband, who has apparently stolen his wife's magic amulet.
    - A team of astronauts exploring the subsurface ocean on Jupiter's moon Europa become trapped in a cave inhabited by strange creatures.

- An abused child escapes through a portal to another universe where he or she befriends a magician who specializes in helping children deal with their abusers.

4. Write a synopsis for a mystery story that opens in the following manner

> An elderly woman walked into my office. "Detective Tanner?"
> "That's me."
> "You're going to think I'm nuts, but the man who claims to be my husband and who looks like my husband is an imposter."

5. Finish drafting the mystery story that begins as follows:

> Corinthian College, its colonial style buildings surrounded by oak and birch trees, lost something of its idyllic luster as several police cruisers filled its main drive. For the third day in a row, a professor had been found dead in her office. All three were female.

6. Brainstorm for a fantasy flash tale set in a land where people can fly, or where people travel on flying horses or dragons, or . . .?
7. Start making plans for a love story between two persons of very different personalities, but who share a very important trait in common. How will that one trait compensate for their personality differences? What steps do one or both of them take to "adjust" their respective personalities? What obstacles must they overcome?
8. Practice writing six-word flash tales that convey a sharp message. For example, I wrote this after reading about yet another child accidentally killed by a gun in the house.

Let's Pretend
by Fred D. White

It's Daddy's gun. We'll just pretend.

Here are some words to kindle your six-word storytelling imagination:

- grenade
- acrobat
- door
- fuse

- "Abort!"
- leap
- trap

Of course, you don't have to limit yourself to six-word stories! Try building a 250-, 500-, or 1000-word flash story using one or more of these words (or their plural or past-tense variants).

5

Writing Literary Flash Fiction

Sometimes when I get an idea for a flash tale, I don't stop to wonder about which category the story is supposed to fit into; instead, I grab a keyboard or good old-fashioned pen and paper, throw caution to the wind, and start writing. Simplicity! The only problem with that option is the possibility of overlooking particular storytelling strategies more suitable to one category than another. If I find myself working on a horror story, for example, it probably would not be a good idea to spend too much time trying to capture the protagonist's relationships with friends and family unless it bore directly on the plot, which is what horror fiction would be mainly concerned with.

The plunge-right-in, trial-and-error approach to fiction writing may work for some writers, but for most, writing requires planning ahead, especially if it involves creating the kinds of complex characters associated with literary fiction—and that includes literary flash fiction.

What Is Literary Flash Fiction?

Literary fiction, flash or otherwise, is less concerned with plot than genre-based fiction, and more concerned with characters: their states of mind, their emotional needs and behavioral complexities, their reactions to the situations they find themselves in more than the situations themselves. Literary flash, like literary fiction in general, probes the consequences of a character's actions or inactions. Such stories do have plots in the sense that things happen or are revealed; but they do not unfold in any formulaic way, with steadily rising tensions, setbacks, and unexpected twists and turns, while leading inevitably to a climax and resolution.

It may seem like a contradiction in terms to talk about literary flash fiction, but it is possible to achieve both extreme brevity and complexity in a thousand words or fewer. How? By allowing the brevity to *enable* the complexity. This is achieved through indirection—through hints and allusions—rather than any explicit, gradually developing situations that would require several chapters of a novel to render fully. In a literary flash story, it is up to the reader to interpret these hints and allusions, to fill in the blanks. Often, a character's actions (or inactions) in a literary flash tale will leave the reader with more questions than answers.

This chapter will take you through a series of steps that will help you compose a literary flash tale. Later on you will want to establish your own method, one that reflects your individual work habits.

Creating Character Profiles

Because characters are central to literary fiction, you will find it worthwhile to think deeply about human nature, and the kinds of people you want to feature in your flash tales. I recommend devoting a section of your writer's notebook to character profiles. Here you will practice describing characters in ways that reflect their complex personalities, their behaviors and their interactions with others. Consider basing your profiles on the following:

- Formative experiences during childhood and adolescence
- Relationships with parents, siblings
- Early social experiences (school, sports and recreation, parties, charitable activities, first jobs)
- Obsessions and how they may have shaped his or her intellectual or career interests
- Fears, anxieties, traumatic moments
- Physical attributes, and how they may have affected his or her personality and behavior

Try preparing your character profiles in either of two different ways: as an itemized list of attributes or as a narrative. Important: Don't hold back on details that may seem trivial or irrelevant; the winnowing process will come once you actually begin work on the story itself.

Here's an example of each type of profile:

Itemized list profile

Jorie Jones

Age: 20

Ethnicity: African American

Current activities: college senior majoring in astrophysics; practices yoga; plays piano to relax; loves hiking, museums, visiting observatories.

Temperament: Intellectual; even-tempered (except when confronted by those who think women are not cut out to be scientists). Limits her social life to fellow enthusiasts in the sciences.

Conflicts: Pressured by some of her peers to become more involved with social issues. Sometimes gets caught up with too many activities at once.

Weaknesses: Problems with self-confidence, frustrated by her inability to get family members to share her passion for astronomy and physics. Has difficulty sustaining romantic relationships.

Goals: To get more minority students interested in science through Head Start programs.

Narrative profile

Jorie Jones

Jorie loves to spend hours gazing through a telescope, or describing the wonders of the universe to family and friends, but easily becomes frustrated when they do not share her enthusiasm. Jorie does in fact get involved with social issues, but in the context of getting people, especially kids, excited about astronomy. She decides to set up neighborhood star parties, and sets up three telescopes on her terrace, each telescope aimed at a specific planet or star cluster or distant galaxy, and prepares mini-lectures to accompany each viewing. Although she tries to be patient with people who do not understand or appreciate her interest in astronomy, she quickly loses her temper with anyone who harbors preconceptions about what women can or cannot do.

There are times, though, when Jorie's anxieties get the better of her. What kind of teacher will she be if she fails to get others to share her enthusiasm? And perhaps, as her critics insist, she should involve herself in more down-to-earth-matters. When people are out of work or live in poor, crime-infested neighborhoods, how can they get enthusiastic about the stars?

When developing character profiles for literary flash fiction, it would be best not to think about the challenges of conveying the complexities of character in fewer than a thousand words. That challenge comes later, at the drafting stage. A first draft of a flash tale might be—and one could argue *should* be—much longer than a thousand words. When it comes time to work on compressing your story, you will have to prioritize character attributes, and delete all but the most essential elements. But to make certain your choices are shrewd ones, you first need to have your characters as fully delineated as possible in your profiles.

Describing Settings

Flash writers do not have the luxury of long descriptive passages to evoke settings. Rather, they must use the fewest words and phrases capable of doing the job that ten or even fifty times as many words would do. This takes lots of practices, so I advise you to include a section in your writer's notebook, along with character profiles, in which you practice capturing a setting vividly in the fewest possible words.

Let's take a close look at the way I handle both interior and exterior settings in the following flash tale:

Snowrise

by Fred D. White

Light snow had begun dusting the lawn on Christmas Eve morning, adding a veneer of expectation to Audrey's melancholy. It was her first Christmas without Stan. She retrieved Todd, who was busily demolishing the Nativity scene, and set him in front of the living room window. "See the snow, sweetie? Maybe it's a message from heaven."

Todd gurgled and shoved the head of one of the Magi into his mouth. Audrey gently pried it out. "Look at the magical snow, honey. Make a wish!"

Todd retrieved the Magus and smacked it against the window; Audrey nudged him back. "If the snow accumulates, we'll make a snowman."

He twisted out of her grip, lost his balance, and fell against the tree, knocking several ornaments loose. Audrey held him until he stopped wailing. "Make a wish on the snow, Todd. It's magical snow. Make a wish and it will come true."

"Wisshhhh!" Todd flung the Magus across the toy-cluttered room.

The snowfall increased.

Audrey whispered a prayer of thanks to the sky. Later, she would bring Todd outside and help him make a snowman. In the meantime, she had to calm him. She brought him, twisting and yelling, into his bedroom, with its deep gouges in the walls, quickly gathered up the sheets and pillows from the floor, placed Todd on the bed, and began her ritual string of lullabies. In ten minutes he was asleep.

A few hours later, while Audrey sat gazing out at the white landscape, sipping a hot toddy, Todd stumbled from his room, opened the front door and ran outside in his pajamas and bare feet. "Todd, no!" Audrey rushed after him. But before she could grab him, he began waving his arms in crazy patterns. She watched in astonishment as snow rose from the ground, billions of glittering crystals cascading upward, a snowspout swirling, spiraling into . . .

But it wasn't possible: a face!

Audrey brought her hands to her mouth to stifle a cry. The snowface was that of her dead husband. The wind was rapidly blowing the snowface across the sky, stretching it, dissipating it, leaving a distorted smile. She lifted Todd and caressed his red, drooling face. "My beautiful, magical boy," she said.

Todd pointed at the sky. "*Wishhhh!*"

As you may have gleaned from the stark contrast between interior and exterior settings, I wanted the indoor setting to capture the harsh reality of caring for a special-needs child, and the outdoor setting to capture both the mother's and the child's dream-fantasy of a magical world. Setting the time during Christmas reinforces the magic element.

Let's look more closely at the more specific techniques I've employed in this story to convey the "harsh reality" of Audrey's predicament and Todd's erratic behavior. First, I described the snowfall as "adding a veneer of expectation" to Audrey's melancholy. It is her first Christmas without her husband, and in her sorrow she is associating the Christmas Eve snowfall as the harbinger of some revelation or miracle. This being a flash tale, there isn't room to examine the psychological nuances behind Audrey's need to make such an association; I leave it to the reader to reflect on those nuances. Next, I depict Todd's behavior in a way that suggests some kind of mystical undercurrent to his actions—for example, his slapping the magus figure to the window and uttering "Wishhhh!"

Developing a Literary Flash Story from Personal Experience

The stories we write usually have some connection to our lives. When we feel the need to tell it the way it "really" happened, we write a personal-experience essay or a book-length memoir. But sometimes we find it more liberating to fictionalize our experiences. There's a larger theme we wish to convey, or we want to create more suspenseful incidents than what actually happened to us, or we want the drama to unfold in a more intriguing setting. There are numerous reasons why writers turn to fiction to tell stories based on their own experiences.

Such is the case with the following story of mine. Read it first, and then I'll tell you how it came about.

Taylor's States
by Fred D. White

Six-year-old Taylor had a gift for assembling jigsaw puzzles with lightning speed. His parents, Jake and Beatrice, discovered it when, shortly before their divorce, they gave him a puzzle map of the United States—each piece a separate, brightly colored state, even the tiny New England states. Taylor dumped the pieces onto the floor and fondled them, fascinated by their shapes. He also learned their capitals, which Jake pronounced for him: MONT-PILL-YER; DE MOYN. He soon could assemble the country in three minutes, naming each state and capital along the way. After Jake packed up and drove away for good, Taylor threw fistfuls of states against the wall. When his mother tearfully gathered them up, he dumped them out again. Later, he assembled the pieces into a strange new pattern, creating a wildly Disunited States.

After the divorce, Beatrice bragged to friends and neighbors about her son's prodigious ability to recognize each state by its shape alone and how he could name every capital. She even contacted a newspaper editor, who invited them downtown so they could witness and record the feat.

The editor spread out an enormous topographic map of the U.S. with only dotted lines to indicate state borders, told Taylor to point rapidly to whatever state they called out and simultaneously shout the name of its capital. As he did so, cameras flashed. The editor tried to fool him with Ohio and South Carolina (Columbus, Columbia), and with North and South Dakota (Bismarck, Pierre), but failed to do so.

After the photo session, the editor asked Taylor, "What's your secret, kid?"

Taylor shrugged. "I like their shapes." He didn't tell the editor that they reminded him of toys, animals, body parts, furniture. Idaho reminded him of a giraffe; West Virginia of a stomach; Vermont, New Hampshire, Rhode Island, of teeth; Maine of a table lamp; Tennessee of a fish; Montana of a cow; New Jersey of a parade cadet; Arkansas of a toilet bowl; Florida of a dog's thingy.

Beatrice bragged to the neighbors about how famous her genius son would become after the feature was published; but the feature never appeared.

Beatrice vented her outrage. "Hell, lady," one neighbor said, "There are six-year-olds who can speak four languages and play Beethoven sonatas!"

But the damage had been done. Taylor's mother's fussing over his prodigious brain had turned him into a snob in spite of himself. He ridiculed classmates who'd never even heard of some states let alone recognize their shapes or know their capitals. They threw water balloons at him. True, some teachers were impressed: "Get him on a quiz show; he'll win thousands!" But other teachers worried that his states-and-capitals performance dampened his enthusiasm for learning other things.

Next year, when Ms. Krupp, Taylor's third-grade teacher, invited her pupils to paint anything their hearts desired, he produced a remarkable likeness of the state of Michigan, complete with Upper Peninsula and surrounding Great Lakes. He painted it bright orange, a more blatant orange than that of the piece from his old puzzle. Nobody he knew had ever lived in Michigan; he merely was fascinated by the way it (Lower Michigan, that is) resembled a boxing glove—a huge Muhammad Ali fist slamming into Canada's mouth.

Not only did Krupp not compliment him on his stupendous cartographical skill, she chastised him for his choice of subjects, her breath reeking of sour milk. "What on earth," she demanded, "prompted you to paint a *state?*"

Taylor could only shrug. It was what he had felt like painting, what he was able to paint best.

"Were you born there?"

"No, ma'am."

"Some relative then."

"Uhm, no, ma'am."

She pressed her dry lips together. "A friend? A former neighbor?"

Shrug.

From then on, Taylor renounced all exhibitions of knowledge. Memorizing state capitals and U.S. Presidents in chronological order, or sports statistics, or pi to twenty decimal places now seemed like a waste of brain cells.

But renunciations were one thing, breaking habits another. Taylor memorized things in spite of himself: the Periodic Table, the constellations, the stars that made up the constellations, all of the geological eras and their constituent epochs, and so on *ad nauseam*.

One day Taylor's fourth grade teacher, Mr. Folsom, called Beatrice to tell her that her son was being transferred to Special Ed. She told Folsom to do something physically impossible with his head; but Taylor was transferred to Special Ed anyway, and the next day found himself face to face with Mr. Winseth, a rodent-eyed man who parted his glossy yellow-brown hair precisely down the middle, and whose fingers wiggled as he spoke. "You shall do exactly what you are told to do in this class," he announced in a shrill voice after hammering his desk with a yardstick.

Winseth emphasized oral recitation, which Taylor loathed. He was worse than Taylor's father, who'd made him memorize hymns for church.

Perversely, Taylor continued to dwell upon the states, on ways he could reshape them with modeling clay. He transformed Oklahoma's skinny panhandle into a coiled elephant's trunk, Nebraska's squat panhandle into a pig's snout, Kentucky into a camel.

By the time he entered fifth grade, he began writing children's stories—stories about the states of the Union coming to life and breeding until there were Tennessee-shaped garfish and Massachusetts-shaped lobsters and fat Texas-shaped turkeys romping about. Daddies would have a wonderful time reading about these crazily shaped states to their children. And the children would laugh, and they would hug their daddies tightly.

—first published in *Five 2 One Magazine*, Jan. 2017; Web.

The germ of this story was sparked by an experience from my early childhood: I liked to play with a map puzzle of the United States, worked it so many times, and became so fascinated by the shapes of the states that I learned their capitals—hard to avoid, since each state/puzzle-piece had the capital printed on it alongside a star with a circle around it. Everything else in the story, though, is fictional or fictionalized (true, my parents divorced, but that came later; and no, I did not, at the time, associate the shapes of the states with objects Taylor associates them with in the story).

Conceptual Flash Fiction

Some literary flash stories illustrate an abstract concept in a clever way, using characters as the means for conveying the cleverness. Take the following tale, for example:

Marriage
by Anna Lea Jancewicz

When she was waiting tables, she used to marry the ketchup bottles. That's what they called it, marrying. Taking two bottles that are less than full, making them one. But the joke was on her.

She figured the punchline while the veil was perched on her head like a ghost sparrow. While she was still waiting on him, off on a beer run with the best man, sure he had at least thirty minutes to burn before he had to hit the altar. But it was too late by then, the dress like a Portuguese man-o-war and the fifty-six chicken dinners were bought and paid for.

It's not like there's this third bottle. There's the bottle with the least left to give, upended. And then that bottle is empty, the other gets it all.

—from *matchbook lit mag.*, Aug. 2014;
reprinted in *The Best Small Fictions* 2015.

Such a strange analogy that Jancewicz uses for marriage—the merging of ketchup! It makes me think of John Donne's poem "The Flea," which celebrates the comingling of the lover's and the beloved's blood inside the flea's belly. The comingling theme goes further to include the sacred and the profane, the sublime and the ridiculous. What does that tell us about the way some people think about matrimony in today's world?

It is also possible to write conceptual literary flash with the characters only in the background, while in the foreground a situation plays out that blurs the distinction between reality and illusion, which is what I attempted in the following tale:

A Shooting in Santa Monica
by Fred D. White

> Production trailers line Pacific Avenue; lighting and sound equipment is strewn along the beachfront, morning mist obscuring the sea; cables crisscrossing the sidewalks; crew people in baseball caps dart back and forth, hollering, some of them with megaphones. Ah, Santa Monica. Many onlookers, myself included, gravitate toward a side street where two guys on either side of a steep-sloping driveway yell something about the take being just about ready for shooting. Several moments later: "ACTION!" and a scrappy two-toned Oldsmobile from the late '50s comes tearing up the driveway, leaping and slamming onto the street. Its rear end fishtails as it shrieks around the corner just as another car—a tail-finned DeSoto—comes within inches of slamming into the Olds. Now gunfire. But the shots are not coming from the take; they're coming from behind me, from somewhere near the Farmer's Market a block away; and now people are screaming and the crowd scatters, like in a *Godzilla* panic scene. Some are running into the street where a second take is being arranged, and one of the assistant directors notices us, takes several lurching *what-the-hell?* steps toward us, toward the screams which are now punctured by more gunfire. Other crew members have caught on. They infiltrate us with their arsenal of cameras.

As you may have guessed, the story hinges on wordplay—the double meaning of "shooting." Word play, as I'll discuss in Chapter 6, is an important technique for humorists and satirists. But it can certainly be used for serious fiction as well. The story also highlights the potential ambiguity that can exist between illusion and reality—an ambiguity especially indicative of moviemaking, as Nathanael West captured with savage irony in his classic novel, *The Day of the Locust* (1939).

Crafting a Literary Flash Story

The steps below are basically the same as the ones that I presented in Chapter 4, but the approach to each step is somewhat different. Let me remind you, as I did when introducing steps for crafting a genre flash story, that the steps can be rearranged, depending on your temperament. However, I recommend that you first follow the seven steps in the sequence given below if you are new to flash fiction writing.

Step One: Brainstorm

When brainstorming for a literary flash tale, start with the people you want to put into the story. Notice that I said "people," not "characters," as the latter term sometimes connotes contrivance. In literary fiction you want the people in your story to seem as authentic as possible—complex, identifiable, flawed. Now imagine these persons at odds with each other. It could be something lurking under the surface, causing tension in their relationship, something neither of them is able to articulate. Or it could be a clash of personalities, temperaments. Think of Felix and Oscar in Neil Simon's famous play, *The Odd Couple* (1966). I bring up Neil Simon because he once described his method of coming up with the premise for a play by imagining two people with seemingly irreconcilable differences thrown into a situation together. I find this to be applicable to writing flash fiction as well.

Step Two: Write the gist of the story in one or two sentences

Remember that your focus is on the people in your story, not the plot. "Two people with radically different tastes and temperaments must find a way to live together for the benefit of both of them" might serve as the premise for *The Odd Couple*. You might want to write a flash tale about two college roommates who must find a way to live together because they both share a fascination with . . .

Another kind of literary flash story would focus not so much on clashing differences as on, say, the romance a married couple vowed to keep alive no matter what; or on the efforts of a manager to downsize without having to lay off her dedicated employees.

Step Three: Write a synopsis

A synopsis adds specific story details to the "gist" sentence(s). Let's work with the above premise: "Two people with radically different tastes and temperaments [how do their tastes and temperaments differ?] must find a way to live together [by doing what?] for the benefit of both of them [how will they benefit?]"

Let's look at another synopsis, the one I worked up for "Snowrise": "A widow grieving for her dead husband wishes for the Christmas season to bestow something magical upon her and her unruly special-needs son. To her astonishment, she discovers that her son is the conduit for that magic."

Step Four: Draft the story

Once you've conjured up the people in your story who are going to clash on some level, it's time to pick up pen and paper and start writing. I recommend that you regard this rough draft as a *discovery* draft because you will inevitably discover things as you're writing. In other words, the act of writing itself stimulates your storytelling imagination. That is why you should allow your storytelling imagination to work unimpeded by switching off the pesky internal editor in your brain (left over, most likely, from your school days). Your internal pesky editor will insist you worry about sentence structure and word choice while your storytelling imagination *wants to tell the story.*

Step Five: Read the story aloud

Reading a literary story aloud may be more of a challenge than reading a genre story aloud, where the question in listeners' minds will be "what's going to happen next?" But listeners can be just as enthralled by character subtleties as readers, provided you make the traits psychologically or behaviorally intriguing. Perhaps your narrator has a volatile temper; perhaps he or she slips into a fantasy world or is so obsessed with moments in the past that the present begins to seem less real (think of Willy Loman in Arthur Miller's *Death of a Salesman*). If you can enthrall listeners with your literary characters, you will certainly enthrall your readers too.

Step Six: Take a "reflection" break

This may not sound like a "step," but it is: those who study the psychology of creativity refer to it as the incubation period, the space your brain needs to acquire aesthetic distance, objectivity. Go do something else for the rest of the day. Come back to your draft the next morning and read it over carefully, making marginal notes. Likelier than not, you will have gained additional insights into your work in progress.

Step Seven: Revise

F. Scott Fitzgerald occasionally, as he put it, revised from spirit—that is, he rewrote the story from scratch without looking back at the original. This should be somewhat easier to do with a flash story. Your goal here is to revisit your characters' motives and behavior, the way you set the scene, the dialogue exchanges, the outcome.

Of course, revision more commonly involves taking an acceptable-enough first draft and improving readability (e.g., making your sentences more concise and readable, your paragraphs more coherent, your word-choice more precise), as well as adding additional concrete details where needed to more effectively tell your story.

Now It's Time to Pick Up Your Pen

1. Joyce Carol Oates writes, "I have always been interested in writing about people who are unable to speak for themselves." In a single paragraph, create a profile of a character who is unable to speak for him- or herself.
2. Write a one-paragraph synopsis of a flash tale featuring the character you profiled in #1 above.
3. Describe a setting through the eyes of a soldier about to enter combat in that setting, which can be an actual place or one that you make up.
4. Write a one-paragraph synopsis of a flash tale about the soldier you profiled in #3. Focus on the soldier's state of mind.
5. Draft a flash story about the soldier you've created in #3 and #4 above.
6. Prepare profiles for five or more characters who will serve as the narrators or protagonists in future flash tales. Use either the list format or the narrative format.
7. Describe two settings that might be incorporated into a single story—one indoors, the other outdoors. You may want to highlight the contrast between the two (as in "Snowrise"), or you may want to suggest subtle similarities.
8. List several concepts you might use as the basis for conceptual flash tales similar to that of "Marriage," above. Next, write a one-sentence premise for each one. In the coming days, develop each of these premises into a 250–500 word flash tale.
9. Make a list of characters based loosely on people you know. Ascribe special attributes to each character (an unusual talent, or a striking

behavioral characteristic). Now write a sentence describing how that talent or characteristic can be used as the basis for a flash story.

10. Select two of the characters from the profiles you prepared for #9; work up a synopsis for a flash tale in which these two characters interact, either as partners or adversaries, in the context of attaining an objective important to both of them. For example, they are co-workers both competing for a promotion.
11. Using the seven-step procedure discussed in this and previous chapters, begin work on flash story centered around a teenager with a physical disability. How does the disability affect her social life? To what extent is she able to overcome the limitations imposed by her disability?
12. Write a flash story in which the distinction between illusion and reality becomes blurred. Here are two possible scenarios for you to work with:
    a. Two or more friends engaging in a role-playing game (e.g., hero vs. villain; hunter vs. hunted), gradually realize they are no longer playing a game.
    b. Actors in a play discover that they have literally become the characters they are portraying.
13. Draw from personal experience to compose a flash story about an adult character who is haunted by a traumatic experience from childhood. Keep in mind that you do not want to write autobiographically, but to use the techniques of flash fiction writing to depict a complex character facing a predicament, a character who will resolve (or attempt to resolve) that predicament in the context of his or her childhood experience. For example, let's say you had a near-drowning experience as a child. Write a flash story in which your adult protagonist must struggle to overcome his or her near-drowning experience to save someone from a shark attack. Draw from the memory of your near-drowning incident (did you panic? what specifically did you do? what went through your mind?) to impart authenticity to your protagonist's feelings and actions.

6

Writing Humorous or Satirical Flash Fiction

No one can be taught to be funny, I suppose; but that doesn't mean there aren't some basic principles of humor writing one can learn in order to start writing and publishing humorous or satirical fiction. People love to laugh, and love to be enlightened through humor; and if you can write funny stuff, you'll soon have a following.

Humor and satire cut across the other flash fiction types I've covered in previous chapters. A humorous story can fall into a traditional genre (humorous science fiction or romance, for example), or humor can be literary, evoking insightful truths of human nature by way of characters who make fools of themselves, say, or who behave in ways that contradict their reputation, such as a tough guy afraid of the dark, or an athlete unable to swim. Modern-day parables or fairy tales can be humorous as well, or can be given modern-day humorous adaptations like David Fisher's *Legally Correct Fairy Tales* (the title of one of the tales being "Petition for Guardianship and Other Legal Relief in the Matter of Beauty, Sleeping"). In any case the trick with literary flash humor is to be both subtle and witty.

Defining "Humor" and "Satire"

Before considering a procedure for composing humorous flash stories, let's first distinguish between humor and satire:

Humor

If something you write makes people laugh (inwardly or outwardly), you've written humor. It can be a joke, of course, but the kind of humor we're dealing with here is storytelling humor: characters in an offbeat situation who resort to offbeat tactics in order to resolve the situation. The more offbeat the situation and the efforts to resolve it, the funnier the story. The humor exists mainly to delight, although not all humor triggers belly laughs. The author often is taking jabs at human foibles, but it's all in the spirit of light-hearted, good fun that leaves us with a feel-good attitude toward the characters.

Satire

The aim of satire is to criticize, to expose corruption, hypocrisy, and many other societal flaws—and to do so wittily. Satirists attack unethical and immoral behavior, especially among those who present themselves as exemplars of good conduct.

Satire has been an effective tool since ancient times. The second-century Roman satirist, Juvenal, for example, lampooned public immorality and folly. Some of the greatest satires in English were written during the eighteenth century, Alexander Pope and Jonathan Swift being the supreme practitioners. In "A Modest Proposal" (1729), Swift's brilliantly caustic response to corrupt mercantilism (that is, the assertion that low wages would *eliminate* poverty because people would be motivated to work harder), Swift proposes that the suffering could easily be alleviated by preparing the children (who would starve to death otherwise) as food. Among the "advantages": "The poorer tenants will have something valuable of their own . . . and help to pay their landlords rent, their corn and cattle being already seized, *and money a thing unknown*."

The Humorist's and Satirist's Toolbox

Regardless of the kinds of flash humor or satire you wish to write, there are several techniques you'll want to become familiar with:

- Irony (saying one thing but meaning its opposite)
- Reversal of expectations (a type of irony—depicting or suggesting outcomes the opposite of what anyone anticipated)
- Language play (puns, malapropisms, double-entendres)
- Reductio ad absurdum (following a bad idea to its logical absurdity)
- Hyperbole (exaggeration for comic effect)
- Understatement (opposite of hyperbole; deflating a momentous event or phenomenon for comic effect)

- Non-sequiturs and other unexpected juxtapositions (interjecting thoughts that have no logical connection to what proceeded; putting objects that are radically unrelated side by side for comic effect)
- Shockingly blunt or wildly out-of-context statements (another type of unexpected juxtaposition)

Let's take a look at some examples of how each of these techniques can be applied in flash humor.

Irony

Oedipus vows to avenge the death of Laertes, unaware at the time that he himself was the murderer, and that Laertes was his own father; Marc Anthony mock-praises Brutus (Caesar's assassin) by saying he is an honorable man; a huge man has nicknamed himself "Tiny"; that unforgettable scene in the 1960 film *Spartacus*, when Spartacus and his friend Antoninus, forced to fight to the death, try to kill each other not out of enmity but of love, to save the other from the agony of crucifixion.

Reversal of expectations

Women smoking cigars; a bully who brags that he can beat up the toughest guys in the school gets decked by a frail-looking kid trained in martial arts; a panhandler who gives money to a passer-by when he learns that the passer-by is a schoolteacher (that last example being the basis for a 1999 "Grand Avenue" comic strip).

Language play

Bud Abbott and Lou Costello's famous "Who's on First?" routine in which "Who" and "What" are baseball players' names as well as pronouns; comedian Bill Maher's captions to the "New Rules" segment on his show; for example, referring to annoying church bells as "Chime and Punishment" (from Maher's book *The New New Rules*).

Reductio ad absurdum

Someone claims that the more active you are the happier you will become. Carried to its absurd but logical conclusion, prisoners sentenced to hard labor would be among the happiest people in the world.

Hyperbole

If it keeps raining like this, we'll have to build an ark; without your love I will shrivel up and die. Remember from your English lit. class that satirical (and naughty) carpe diem poem, "To His Coy Mistress," by the seventeenth century poet Andrew Marvell?

Had we but world enough, and time,
This coyness, lady, were no crime.
We would sit down, and think which way
To walk, and pass our long love's day

An hundred years should go to praise
Thine eyes, and on thy forehead gaze;
Two hundred to adore each breast,
But thirty thousand to the rest . . .

Understatement

After an actor receives a wild standing ovation, someone says, "I think they liked him"; Woody Allen's joke, "Eternal nothingness is OK if you're dressed for it" (from *Getting Even*).

Non-sequiturs and other unexpected juxtapositions

In my story "The Great Camilla" (Chapter 3), an infant cusses when the magician Camilla accidentally drops him.

Shockingly blunt or wildly out of context statements

Hamlet and Ophelia, Macbeth and Lady Macbeth double-date in a modern-day steakhouse in Peter Cherches's "Double Date" (Chapter 3).

Using Flash Humor to Poke Fun at Our Modern Age

Humor and satire are plentiful in our time—and it's no wonder, with all the fiery politics and the continuous avalanche of technology affecting our daily lives. If you want material for humorous or satirical flash, just pick up or log on to your favorite newspaper or cable news show—or better yet, think about the advances in social-media and entertainment technology. To cite a personal example, one day I was reading about all the smartphone apps currently available and wondered, yes—but what about smartphone *accs*? (a term I coined on the spot). Before long, I began working on what eventually became the following piece:

E-Reader Accessories for the Terminally Indolent
by Fred D. White

"The shift to digital books has fueled an arms race among digital start-ups seeking to cash in on the massive pool of data collected by e-reading devices and reading apps."
—Alexandra Alter, "Your E-Book Is Reading You," A&E, July 19, 2012.

While e-reader manufacturers struggle to make sense of the reading habits of more than a hundred million digital-device enthusiasts (40 million e-readers and 65 million tablets are in use, according to Ms. Alter), little or no attention is being given to the growing frustration with even the most sophisticated devices: they still have to be held in most situations. If we're going to forego the sensory delights of physical books, we should at least encourage development of innovative accessories that will remedy this problem. The following accs should please even the most indolent e-book lover:

The H- (Head or Hat) Acc: Bound to ignite a new fashion trend, the head acc tethers the e-reader to the top of the skull (like a beanie with a sloping tether), or to the bill of a baseball cap. The tether is sturdy yet flexible enough to permit reading at any angle—up, down, straight ahead, or sideways. (Those who prefer to read on their sides, take note: this acc can be stretched to twice its length to permit reading off the hip.) And as you rhythmically thumb the pages, you'll set the h-reader a-swaying, gently enough to make you sleepy.

The F- (Foot) Acc: Sometimes the snazziest innovations are hidden in plain sight, just like one's feet while reading in bed. This simple peda-clip-on acc will enable any reader (especially far-sighted ones) to stretch out on the bed or sofa and foot-read, even with the feet covered. Yes, you'll have to bend forward to change pages, but just think of the workout you'll be giving your flabby abs when doing so!

The O- (Omphalos) Acc: Named for Zeus's umbilical cord, this belly-hugging reading acc comprising three flexible flying buttresses lets your e-reader sit comfortably on your midriff. Ideal for anyone wishing to read with legs propped on a desk, or splayed on a hassock or in a hammock, or even while leg pedaling.

The N-T-H (Not Tonight, Honey) Acc: This welcome e-reader accessory clips to the recharger cord, which one then coils around your beloved's waist while he or she is either facing toward or away from you (preferably the latter). A good time to slip it on is during or immediately after spooning. Also, the N-T-H acc has a vibrating option (speeds vary) to soothe both you and your partner as you page with bated breath through the latest Jack Reacher thriller.

The D-T-E (Direct-To-Eyeball) Acc: This is fringe, no doubt, destined to make Google Glass (the image-accessing program you wear like a pair of glasses) seem quaint by comparison. The D-T-E acc release date may be delayed, pending further testing; but I've seen a prototype and it is, well, eye-popping. The acc consists of electrodes in the guise of contact lenses which are placed directly over the pupils; the electrode wires connect to the e-reader. The text thus occupies your entire field of vision. Now here is what's

> most clever about this acc: One turns the pages by blinking twice. Of course, anyone suffering from spasmodic blinking, or even blinking more than twice per second, will be obliged to quadruple his or her reading speed—but, as is the case with the foot-acc, it would be a blessing in disguise.
>
> Additional e-reader accessories will almost certainly appear on the market once the terabytes of data on e-reading habits are thoroughly mined, new NSA directives notwithstanding. Marketers and investors are interested in the peculiar reading habits of e-text consumers insofar as they intertwine with contiguous habits such as lounging, napping, or gazing into space. It has been theorized that reading is as much a physical act as a cognitive one; hence, these suggested accessories are likely to make digital reading an even more pleasurable experience than print-book reading, especially when one considers how previously overlooked portions of the anatomy may now be made part of the reading experience. At the very least, these accs should make the retro-head fuddy-duddies think twice about accusing e-reader manufacturers of alienating humanity from the sensory pleasures of print.
>
> —first published in *Clockwise Cat* #29 (October 2017). Web.

As you can see, I used several techniques from the toolbox: hyperbole, unexpected juxtapositions, language play, and *reductio ad absurdum.*

How to Write a Humorous or Satirical Flash Tale

One can't force humor. You may love to read humorous stories, but you yourself may not be inclined to write them. My advice: read through this chapter anyway and see if your inclination changes. It can happen!

As with the other steps in Chapters 4 and 5, the ones that follow are similar, but they include variations specific to humor writing.

Step 1: Brainstorm for an appropriate topic.

Think about incidents you've experienced, and how they might be rendered humorously or satirically, being mindful of the techniques available in the humorist's/satirist's toolbox (irony, language play, hyperbole, etc.). For starters, focus sharply on the target issue. Do that (a) by writing out your grievance with the issue in a single sentence; next (b), list all the specific reasons why you think the issue is worthy of lampooning, of poking fun at; finally (c), concoct a scenario that would demonstrate the folly of the target issue.

Step 2: Write the gist of your humor piece in one or two sentences

I suggest that you try to capture the gist of the story (the premise) in the very first sentence. Then, in the second sentence, convey a humorous element. For example, to use the "shockingly blunt" technique from the toolbox:

"Johnny hated his stepmother's cooking, but couldn't think of a polite way to convey his feelings. And then, one day, he puked up his dinner right at the table." By the way, note how this distillation of the piece essentially sets the tone of the story.

Step 3: Expand your "gist" sentence into a one-paragraph synopsis

To use Johnny's problem with his stepmother's cooking, expand the sentence to include Johnny's plan to solve the problem. Perhaps it's to recruit a neighbor or a sibling to help in the kitchen (which may lead to even more culinary mayhem).

If your aim is satire, though, the paragraph should focus on, say, the stepmother's unwillingness to face the reality of her lack of cooking skill and her efforts to blame others for their lack of appreciation for the meals she prepares.

Step 4: Draft the story

For either humor or satire, use a format to facilitate the drafting, such as script format, especially if you're thinking in terms of a *Saturday Night Live*-type comedy sketch. Here's an example of script format from a Marx Brothers comedy:

> MRS. TEASDALE: As chairwoman of the reception committee, I welcome you with open arms.
>
> GROUCHO: Is that so? How late do you stay open?
>
> MRS. TEASDALE: I've sponsored your appointment because I feel you are the most able statesman in all Freedonia.
>
> GROUCHO: Well, that covers a lot of ground. Say, you cover a lot of ground yourself.
>
> —from *Duck Soup*

By the way, note the scriptwriter's use of language play—a favorite comic device of the Marx Brothers.

Step 5: Read or enact the story aloud

You can't fake laughter (well, you can, but it sounds fake)—so reading your humorous fiction aloud to a group of people would be a surefire way of testing it. Of course, you'll need to endure the embarrassment if no one laughs.

If you're writing your flash humor piece as a script, have fun by assigning roles to friends.

Step 6: Take a "reflection" break

One of the hazards of writing humor is forcing the humor or satire, or drawing from old material without realizing it at the time. As you reflect on the draft of your flash tale, ask yourself if the wit is genuine and original, and if the wit conveys the serious underlying premise effectively enough.

Step 7: Revise!

That exclamation mark is not gratuitous. Writing is thinking on paper, and thought is by its very nature complex because it must orchestrate language—a system of abstract, arbitrary symbols—to convey reality (subjective or objective). Words very rarely come out right the first time. I can't help but think that if we spent more time mulling over our oral everyday discourse (i.e., revising in our heads), we would get along so much better. So, plan your revisions carefully and patiently. See my pointers regarding revision in Chapter 4.

Cases-in-Point: A Close Look at a Satirical and a Humorous Flash Tale

Let's look at a couple examples, both of them (ahem) my own. The first, "Bremer in Extremis," is an academic satire—and in case you haven't looked at my biographical note, I've been a university professor for thirty-one years (and a community college instructor for several years before that), so I have lots of satirical stories to tell about life in the academy.

The second piece, "A Horoscope for the Astronomically Minded," is more humorous than satirical in that I thought it would be funny to imagine what it would take for people who prefer science to pseudoscience to become interested in astrology.

First, the satire:

Bremer in Extremis

by Fred D. White

Professor Karl Bremer walked rapidly from his office to Gottlieb Hall to teach his poetry class. He was early, as usual; he enjoyed chatting informally with the students. As he crossed the campus, he kept his head down to avoid eye contact with colleagues, especially administrators like the Dean of Liberal Arts or the Provost or the Vice President for Academic Affairs or the Associate Vice Provost for Faculty Development or—God forbid—the Department Chair or the Coordinator of First-Year Composition or the Chair of the Curriculum Committee, or any member of the Chair's Executive

Committee. He'd resolved not to be yoked to yet another ad hoc committee or task force; after all, his mental health was at stake.

Bremer glared at the recently constructed building looming ahead: Gottlieb Hall, new headquarters for the Ernst Gottlieb School of Business, where his poetry classes had been assigned—vindictively, he couldn't help suspect. Gottlieb's classrooms were lecture halls with terraced, bolted-down seats, odious whiteboards, and state-of-the-art computer projection systems that Bremer never used, despite the Chair's mandate that department faculty cut back on photocopying, if nothing else. Bremer had repeatedly requested classrooms in old Jaspers Hall (the traditional venue for English classes), with its threadbare carpeting, chalkboards, and wobbly but moveable chairs that made small-group interaction so much easier.

Bremer struggled to preserve his faith in academe as the last best hope of humankind despite the changes that were taking place more rapidly than he could assimilate. But today he felt overwhelmed, and was tempted to cancel his remaining class, his office hours, and spend the rest of the day meditating.

But his pragmatic side prevailed. Inside Gottlieb Hall, Bremer swiftly climbed the metal stairs to his classroom. Students were spilling into the corridors, phones pressed to their ears. Several students nearly collided with him.

Poetry! Auden's "the clear expression of mixed feelings"; Frost's "a way of remembering what would impoverish us to forget."

Today they would discuss T.S. Eliot's "The Love Song of J. Alfred Prufrock." Poor Prufrock, leeched of joie de vivre, imprisoned by his own incapacitated psyche. *What a loser*, his students will say. Carpe diem!

> The clock keeps ticking, honey, so unhook your bra.
> No patient etherized upon a table, moi!

Bremer took a deep breath. It was time to ruffle students' feathers; time to unbolt the seats, time to smash the overhead projection system. The clock was ticking! Time to pay homage to the Muses; carpe diem indeed! Time to transform this well-endowed but anal-retentive Gottlieb Hall into a den of aesthetic iniquity. Time to disturb the universe!

Professor Karl Bremer whispered his teaching prayer, and opened the classroom door.

—first published in *Praxis Literary Journal*, May 2016. Web.

How I wrote "Bremer in Extremis"

Being a teacher of writing as well as a writer, I keep a composition log of some of my own stories. Sometimes a story, even a flash story, comes to fruition only after years of incubation. Such was the case with "Bremer in Extremis." I am not a technophobe or a Luddite; but even so, I found myself losing patience with what I considered to be an over-reliance on technology in the humanities. On top of that, I'd been also losing patience with excessive bureaucracy in academe. One day it occurred to me that excessive bureaucracy was not unlike excessive technology: both tended to interfere with physical (as opposed to cyber) human interrelationships. And that was how I got the idea for this story.

The first thing I did was jot down snippets of things that were beginning to strike me as silly or pretentious or downright absurd about academe—most obvious (to me at least) being the penchant for over-determined academic roles. Next, I searched my humorist's toolbox possible for techniques, and chose hyperbole to draw attention to what strikes me as the sometimes excessive bureaucracy of academe, and unexpected juxtaposition to highlight the incongruity (or what should be regarded as incongruity) between the narrator's desire for small-group interaction and the bolted-down seats.

Now for the humor piece:

A Horoscope for the Astronomically Minded
by Fred D. White

Asking people what sign they're under might make for lighthearted party banter; but most agree that astrology has no basis in reality. The planets, let alone stars, are too distant to exert any degree of influence (gravitational or otherwise) on one's destiny or temperament. Still, many continue to be charmed by the thought that their destinies are governed by celestial forces. Astronomical facts just aren't compelling enough to dispel that longing.

But compromise is possible! Welcome to the New Astrology, whereby the astronomical discoveries of the past half-century have finally had an influence on the venerable pseudoscience. No more balderdash about the Moon entering the Seventh House or bellicose Mars looping ominously through peaceful Aquarius. There are now new signs that are certain to resonate with younger generations, especially those who have taken Intro to Astronomy during their sophomore year. To wit:

SUMBLAC, the Super-Massive Black Hole lurking at the center of our galaxy, replacing Aries the Ram (March 21–April 18): As a Sumblac, you tend to be both elusive and aggressive. Expect to be victorious with hostile takeovers. Competitors will try to steer clear of you, but your influence will predominate. Keep in mind, however, that such predominance in the business world may undermine your trustworthiness.

KUBO, the Kuiper-Belt Object; formerly Taurus the Bull (April 20–May 20): Kubos tend to struggle with an inferiority complex, yet always manage to regain their self-esteem. Like Pluto, once a noble Planet, now reclassified as a Kuiper Belt Dwarf Planet, you are destined to attain a high position in your career, only to be demoted through no fault of your own. But because you are blessed with a resilient nature, you will not let setbacks get the better of you. Indeed, a lawsuit could work in your favor.

DOBS, the Double Star, formerly Gemini Twins (May 21–June 21): If you're a typical Dobs, you know what it's like to go through life being shadowed by an envious, less enterprising sibling, one who is always looking for ways to undermine or take credit for your accomplishments. You will discover ingenious ways of retaining your status as the Alpha in the family.

CORBOP, the Cosmic Ray Bombardment Phenomenon; formerly Cancer the Crab (June 22–July 22): You are possessed of enormous energy, which tends either to inspire or intimidate others. Like your Sign, which, according to astrophysicists, emanates from the Big Bang itself, your energy levels are inexhaustible and can reach levels of near-lethal intensity. Never lose sight of your powers, or you could harm the ones you love.

SOFIA, the Stratospheric Observatory for Infrared Astronomy, formerly Leo the Lion (July 23–August 22): Pride and independent mindedness are the dominant Sofian traits. No one pulls the wool over your eyes! Such vigilance has made you into an astute observer, not only of people but of natural (especially celestial) phenomena. The only sign in the astronomically informed New Astrology that is an artifact, Sofia will guide your destiny as an engineer and versatile handyperson who will never fall prey to unscrupulous mechanics.

POCREA, the Pillars of Creation, formerly Virgo the Virgin (August 23–September 22): As a Pocrea, you are fertile of mind and body. Like Venus rising out of the sea on a half-shell, you project purity mingled with earthiness and coupled with the promise of the kind of fertility that can spawn a dynasty of high achievers. Find some way to connect your unsullied demeanor with your earthier innermost self, or risk the loss of an extraordinary destiny.

DARMAT, Dark Matter, (formerly Libra, Scales, September 23–October 23): Darmats want to be inconspicuous, ideally invisible, yet at the same time wish to pursue activities that require collaboration. How you progress will hinge upon your ability to find a middle ground between these contradictory traits. Hint: give equal consideration to contradictory points-of-view. Remember that your success hangs in the balance.

LOPOC, the long-period Oort Cloud Comet (formerly Scorpio, the Scorpion, October 24–November 21): If you prefer to remain out of the limelight, you are a typical Lopoc. True, you occasionally get the urge to appear unannounced at social events; but in general, you are even-tempered, content to scuttle along the outskirts of life. It will be in your best interest this coming holiday season to avoid crashing parties—you could get stung.

WORHOL, the Wormhole, formerly Sagittarius, the Archer (November 23–December 21): Aside from getting inexplicable urges to paint soup cans, you are a genius at figuring out shortcuts to difficult problems. A straight shooter, you insist on being blunt in your relations with friends and associates. Maintain this reputation; it will bring you a rich bounty.

CORMAJ, a Coronal Mass Ejection Event, formerly Capricorn the Goat (December 22–January 19): Cormajes are hot-tempered. Often a fate-sealer, such a trait is one that you can control by avoiding the urge to butt into other people's business. You are apt to capitalize on the ease with which you can intimidate others just by your very presence.

GLEISE, the Red Dwarf Star Gleise 876, in the constellation Aquarius; bearer of a planetary system including the super-earth Gleise 876-d; formerly Aquarius the Water Bringer (January 20–February 18): Nobody truly can understand you, and that is how you like it. You convey intrigue, possibility; friends do all they can to get you to reveal more of yourself. Stay mysterious! It will ensure peaceful interactions. When invited to receptions, bring libations.

ETAQ, the Cepheid Variable Star Eta Aquilae (formerly Pisces, the Fish, February 19–March 20): Like your sign, a member of a class of stars that enabled modern astronomers to determine cosmic distances, you have a mercurial nature—easily confused with bipolar disorder. Unlike those afflicted with bipolar disorder, though, you can control your emotional extremes: yes, highly agitated—a veritable fish out of water—when faced with new surroundings, but subdued and contemplative among family. During your next sign-period, expect to be swept along in a current of daunting but satisfying challenges.

—first published in *Clockwise Cat* #38; Sept. 2017. Web.

How I wrote "A Horoscope for the Astronomically Minded"

I've been an astronomy nut ever since, as a kid, I visited Griffith Observatory in Los Angeles (where I was born and grew up). Some of my favorite authors are astronomers like Carl Sagan, Dennis Overbye, and Neil de Grasse Tyson, who have written endlessly fascinating books on the mysteries of the cosmos. Astrology, on the other hand, with its origins in ancient times, was humankind's prescientific effort to find a relationship between human beings and the heavens. Knowing such yearning for cosmic connectedness exists even among the scientific minded, I thought that an astronomical rather than an astrological horoscope might just tickle a few funnybones.

So once I came up with the idea for a horoscope format, my next step was to make a list of all the astronomical phenomena I knew about, and then to see if I could link twelve of them to the signs of the zodiac—and was delighted that I could do so. Next, I wondered which techniques I could use from the humorist's toolbox. The first ones that leaped to mind were irony and hyperbole—as if folks who were astronomically minded (as opposed to astrologically minded) would have the slightest interest in horoscopes of any kind. My last predrafting step was to come up with horoscope-sounding names. Once I had those, the drafting came easily.

Now It's Time to Pick Up Your Pen

1. Begin work on a humorous fable. Start by drawing up character profiles of animals who may or may not wind up in your flash tale. They might be farm animals similar to those in George Orwell's *Animal Farm*, or mythical animals (e.g., unicorns, griffins). Review the list of techniques from the humorist's toolbox to spark your creative thinking.
2. Make up your own signs associated with some festivity—your own Twelve Days of Christmas, or your own Chinese *shengxiao*, the twelve animal signs of the Zodiac. Instead of the Year of the Tiger, Rooster, Dog, Dragon, Monkey, etc., imagine what animal signs you can invent, along with personality traits, for laughs.
3. Start keeping a list of puns—of words that have double (sometimes opposite) meanings, and which you might use in a flash piece for comic effect. Think of plays on names of persons and places (e.g., Jerry Lewis's old joke of calling Las Vegas "Lost Wages"). Think of clichés, common phrases, and titles of movies or TV shows (someone I knew who disliked science fiction once referred to the classic science fiction TV series as Star Dreck).
4. One of the purposes of satire is to ridicule individuals or groups of shady or criminal reputations—think of Woody Allen's skewering of mafia figures in "A Look at Organized Crime" where he pokes fun at crime boss's nicknames (e.g., "Dominick (The Herpetologist) Mione." (Ridicule is a form of hyperbole, by the way.) Write a flash piece in

which you satirize an organization you think should be brought down a notch or two. Some possibilities:

- Members of an exclusive country club
- Followers of a religious cult
- Members of a "genius" society like Mensa
- A meeting of crime bosses to discuss reorganization

5. Prepare a dramatic skit using script format. Start with a cast of characters appropriate for the 2–4 page scenario you have in mind; then write a one-sentence premise and expand it into a one-paragraph synopsis. Finally, draft the sketch. Here are a few potentially comedic situations you may want to work with:
   - A patient in a mental hospital tries to convince a nurse that he is perfectly sane.
   - An acting coach tries to get a male student to play a female role (or vice versa)—or (rather more challenging) an insect or mollusk.
   - A physical fitness trainer instructs a trainee.
   - An evolutionary biologist tries to explain evolution to a Creationist—or vice-versa.
   - A dance instructor tries to teach someone with two left feet how to waltz.
6. Write a 2–3-minute carpe diem comedy skit (1 page = 1 minute) in the spirit of Marvell's "To His Coy Mistress."
7. Try your hand at a brief (2–3 pages) political monologue in which you poke fun at two senators or congresspersons from different parties arguing over a timely and controversial issue.
8. Write a two-page flash satire in which you use a fictitious situation (but one that should easily remind readers of an actual one) to lampoon a government official or business executive for one of the following lapses of judgment:
   - Using taxpayer dollars to support a mistress
   - Embezzling company funds to support a drug habit
   - Blissfully ignoring an urgent municipal problem

9. Use a skit from a favorite TV comedy show and transform it into a 1000-word flash tale, without using script format. Remember to review the humorist's/satirist's toolbox for possible techniques.

7

Writing Experimental Flash Fiction

If you are drawn to avant-garde or experimental writing, flash is the ideal medium. Of course, experiments in fiction should be grounded in some purpose, whether it be artistic, poetic, philosophical, thematic, or all of the above, and not be undertaken for its own sake, unless you simply want to have fun writing weird stuff for the heck of it and seeing if it leads to anything substantive. Ideally, experimenting should stretch existing boundaries, explore new ways of thinking about human relationships, or explore new ways of thinking about identity, personality, or the perception of reality itself.

Flash is also ideal for stretching the convention of "text" to include visual elements, including the way words are arranged on the page. Of course, mixing visual elements with text has a long tradition, especially in children's stories; but illustrations sometimes appear in longer fictions, such as the novels of Charles Dickens, Lewis Carroll, and Mark Twain. Experiments with visuals can also include the insertion of diagrams, charts, lists, maps, reproductions of news clippings, and so on within the body of the narrative. Keep in mind, though, that many visual elements, such as photographs, drawings, and paintings, are protected by copyright and permission would be required to reproduce them.

One can also experiment with shifts from prose to poetry (including song lyrics) or even mathematical formulas. Again, if you are using material from another source published within the past 100 years, permission from the copyright owner must be obtained before your story can be published.

Types of Experiments with Flash Fiction

There are many ways to experiment with flash fiction, and more than one way can be incorporated into a single work. You can experiment with:

- length
- subject matter
- metafiction
- characters and viewpoint
- time
- language and style
- intersections of reality and dream (a preoccupation with absurdist writers)

Let's take a close look at each of these modes of experimentation.

Experimenting with Length

The length limit for flash fiction is generally 1000 words or fewer. "Fewer" has opened the door to 100- or 250-word micro-flash, six-word flash (see Chapter 4), and 280-character Twitter flash. These are not arbitrary length limits, but bona fide subgenre categories, each with their own peculiar manner of storytelling. For example, in Jerome Stern's volume of 250-word-maximum stories (most of them almost exactly 250 words) titled *Micro Fiction* (1996), the stories have the lyric properties of poems, but are character-centered as well. Here is an example from the novelist and short-story writer Antonya Nelson:

Land's End

by Antonya Nelson

Her foot begins bleeding on the beach, cut by the jagged funnel of a broken bottle. Cerveza, she thinks, and, also, that her blood is the only thing there belonging to her. Foreign country, driven to in a friend's truck, the shirt she wears from a long-ago lover, crusty no-color shorts found folded in the house, and the house itself, ahead, that belongs to an uncle. Her blood-prints in the sand like valentines.

She's been running again, this time on foot, running south, she's come from unlikely Kansas to the Mexican Gulf, sliding down her own country, gravitating toward the equator. At the border a toothless woman sold her a shrink-wrapped Saint Dymphna, patroness of nervous disorders. She laughed, but uneasily. Did a sane person laugh, all alone? The Mexican had three teeth, no more. Where do all the world's teeth go, she wonders now, hobbling dizzily through the debris, clamshells and plastic bags, praying to her new saint that the roving pack of dogs will not attack her, nor the fishermen, who watch dispassionately from boats, weaving nets of bright green acrylic.

In the house—no tapwater, no windowglass, no easy-chair—she leans against the stove and ties a sock around the wound. On the burner rests a notebook, the entries of former guests, their gratitude for a place to overindulge: sun, drink, sex. She feels excluded by their exclamation marks; she tries to imagine what she might write, tomorrow, what someone like her might have to say after the night ahead.

Outside, the setting sun begins its furor. A trail of red hearts points the way to her. Wild dogs howl.

—first published in *Micro Fiction: An Anthology of Really Short Stories*, ed. Jerome Stern, Norton; 1996. Reprinted by permission of the author.

As for Twitter flash, you can have fun with your mobile phone by sending these 280-character-max stories to friends wherever you happen to be. Here is one of my own:

The Sacrifice

by Fred D. White

The rumbling and shaking keeps getting worse, and people are starting to panic. "What is happening, Father?" my daughter cries. "Fear not," I reply, and hurry out to the market, where I purchase a fat hen—the last one left. I slit its throat on the spot, and raise it to the smoky sky. My own fears ebb as I watch several others do the same.

Surely, the gods will be appeased by this, and Vesuvius will return to sleep.

Experimenting with Subject Matter

Flash fiction writers often improvise with genre conventions such as romance or mystery, coming up with offbeat story situations. For example, two people being treated for schizophrenia fall in love; or a detective with brilliant crime-solving skills is hampered by claustrophobia or his inability to stomach the sight of blood. (Think of Monk, the detective in the TV series, hampered by his extreme OCD.)

One can also experiment with surreal situations—the textual equivalent of a painting by Salvador Dali, Rene Magritte, or Dorothea Tanning—images containing identifiable objects or persons but in bizarre, dreamlike (or nightmare-like) configurations that represent a reality that the mind has repressed because it violates socially acceptable norms or the dreamer's own sense of decorum. In fact, dreams are an ideal resource for experimenting with subject matter. Psychoanalysis, including psychopathology and dream analysis, that took root in the early twentieth century, continues to influence all areas of modern art and literature.

Perhaps the most important influence in fictional experimentation derives from radical changes in culture: new perceptions of race and ethnicity, the immigrant experience, and LGBT rights (borne out of past abuses and misconceptions). These cultural reperceptions have affected all the arts, but writers of flash fiction have the opportunity to share their creative insights via the concentrated (and therefore more aesthetically potent) medium of flash fiction.

Experimenting with Metafiction

Metafiction refers to stories that call attention to themselves as stories. Cinematic forerunners of metafiction are the Marx Brothers and Bob Hope movies, where, for example, Hope looks into the camera and wonders how he got roped into making a movie like this. You sometimes see cartoons in *The New Yorker* magazine using metafiction, as in the cartoon in which two persons marooned on a tiny island see a small boat approaching and one says to the other, "Cartoonists." Metafiction can be an amusing device in flash fiction, provided you use it in a clever way. Like many literary techniques, it can be overused to the point of becoming trite. Here is one of my favorite metafictional flash tales:

The Executive and the Witch

by anonymous

The young executive had taken $100,000 from his company's safe, lost in playing the stock market, and now he was certain to be caught, and his career ruined. In despair, down to the river he went.

He was just clambering over the bridge railing when a gnarled hand fell upon his arm. He turned and saw an ancient crone in a black cloak, with wrinkled face and stringy gray hair. "Don't jump," she rasped. "I'm a witch, and I'll grant you three wishes for a slight consideration."

"I'm beyond help," he replied, but he told her his troubles, anyway.

"Nothing to it," she said, cackling, and she passed her hand before his eyes. "You now have a personal bank account of $200,000!" She passed her hand again. "The money is back in the company vault!" She covered his eyes for the third time. "And you have just been elected first vice-president."

The young man, stunned speechless, was finally able to ask, "What—what is the consideration I owe you?"

"You must spend the night making love to me," she smiled toothlessly.

The thought of making love to the old crone revolted him, but it was certainly worth it, he thought, and together they retired to a nearby motel.

In the morning, the distasteful ordeal over, he was dressing to go home when the old crone in the bed rolled over and asked, "Say, sonny, how old are you?"

"I'm forty-two years old," he said. "Why?"

"Ain't you a little old to believe in witches?"

—first published in *Playboy Magazine*, March 1964; HMH Pub. Co.;
reprinted in *The Dynamics of Literary Response*,
by Norman N. Holland (Oxford U.P., 1968)

What makes this piece so clever is how it exploits our willing suspension of disbelief when reading fairy tales (or any other kind of fiction, for that matter), and then mercilessly pulls readers out of that suspension. This is metafiction on steroids!

Experimenting with Characters (Including Non-Adult Characters) and Viewpoint

Unconventional characters as narrators, conveying radically different ways of perceiving the world, have been around since Cervantes sent Don Quixote chasing after windmills. We have seen the world through mentally challenged narrators (Benjy in William Faulkner's *The Sound and the Fury*; Lenny in John Steinbeck's *Of Mice and Men*), and through the eyes of a slave in the movie *Twelve Years a Slave*. I myself have tried to narrate stories through the eyes of the troubled, oppressed, or marginalized, without judging whether they are "heroes" or "villains." Here is the flash tale I wrote from the point of view of a high-school bully:

The Bully
by Fred D. White

I'm a bully, proud of it. Guys look up to me, which says something because I'm short. But being short don't bother me any longer, and once you lay eyes on me, you'll see why: I got muscular. Punch me in the gut, you'll bruise your knuckles. All I'm missing are tats. Skull tats. Spider tats. Swastika tats. I'd cover myself in tats if this jerk off school would let me. When my bud Josh-O cut a scorpion tat on his neck he got expelled, how anal is that? I'm gonna put a Great White tat, teeth bared, on my gut, so when we shower after gym I'll be able to see who freaks and who awes. The ones that freak will become my next targets—them and the holier-than-thous that barf about the evils of bullying—or the gushy types that say we're victims of abuse and that we deserve to be better understood. True, my old man used to beat the shit out of me if I didn't comb my hair right, and my ma drank herself into an early grave, but I'm a bully because I *like* being a badass. The bleeding hearts can shove their compassion up their asses.

Then there's the phony-baloneys that pretend to ignore me altogether. I hate them most because they're as scared as the freak-outs and even the ass-lickers. Take Berkowitz, who hardly ever talks. The other day I shoulder-punched him just to see how he'd react—but he didn't react at all. I knew damn well he was pretending, like he was telling me I wasn't any scarier than a goddamn chair he bumped into. Well, I decided then and there to go the full Monty with Berkowitz.

One day after school I cornered him and said, "That schnoz of yours is so high in the air, Berko-witzo, someone might come along and break it right off." But he side-stepped me like I was some piece of dog shit. That was when I slugged him—*crack!*—and his nose started gushing blood like a faucet. He just stared at me, blood spilling onto his shirt and shoes. Seeing all that blood made me sick. So much for being a badass.

With his eyes locked onto mine, Berkowitz slowly pulled a handkerchief from his pocket and pressed it against his nose.

I grabbed his arm and blubbered, "Jeezus, Berk-o, I didn't mean to hit you so hard. I was just horsin' around. Forgive me?"

Without a word, he smeared a cross on my forehead with his bloody handkerchief.

The only impulse I felt at the outset (my brainstorming stage) was to see if I could capture what goes through the mind of someone who had earned the reputation of bully or who thought of himself as a bully. The synopsis I jotted down was this:

> High school guy compensates for his shortness by muscling up and being a badass any way he can. What he can't admit to himself, though, is his squeamishness and his longing for acceptance—qualities that emerge unexpectedly when he confronts a potential victim who utterly ignores his bullying actions.

What came to me unexpectedly while trying to come up with a strong ending was the theme of forgiveness (and its religious associations). Berkowitz's act of painting a crucifix on the bully's forehead was his way of indicating that the forgiveness the bully seeks is, as Christianity promises, always available.

Considering that the characters in "The Bully" are adolescents (see also my story "Taylor's States," in Chapter 5), you may be wondering how flash fiction fits in with a younger audience. I for one am uneasy about categorizing flash fiction as "youth flash fiction" merely because the characters are non-adults. True, there is such a thing as young adult (YA) and juvenile fiction, but it relates mainly to novels or (for young children) children's magazine stories and picture books. That said, there exists an anthology of flash fiction featuring non-adult characters, *Flash Fiction Youth.* Here is one chilling example:

The Coat

by Lex Williford

Eighth grade. Mrs. Jaffrey's class. It was always cold in Mrs. Jaffrey's class. It was always freezing in there. And every day I wore my coat to her class she told me not to.

"Why not?" I asked her. "It's cold in here. I'm cold."

"Because you're not supposed to wear your coat to class," she kept saying.

Seemed pretty stupid to me, so I kept wearing my coat to class. I was cold.

After a few days, Mrs. Jaffrey told me to hang my coat up in the principal's office. Told me to stay there for the rest of the afternoon. Told me to write her a five-hundred word essay on why I shouldn't wear my coat to class.

"Why?" I asked her. "I can't do that. How'm I supposed to do that?"

She looked at me over her horn-rims. Her lips were white. She had her arms folded. The north wind coming up off the practice fields outside had glazed the windowpanes along the wall with ice.

"Be creative," she said.

I sat in the principal's warm office and wrote a hundred sentences, like the ones I'd written on the detention hall chalkboard for Mrs. Jaffrey after school.

I will not wear my coat to class because someone might mistake me for a bear and shoot me.

I will not wear my coat to class because I might sweat so much the class will flood, and somebody might drown.

I will not wear my coat to class because I might get so hot I'll catch fire and burn the whole junior high down.

That kind of thing. It was more than five hundred words. I thought it was pretty creative.

Mrs. Jaffrey didn't think so, though. Neither did my old man. Next day, he showed up outside Mrs. Jaffrey's class with my essay in his hand. Checked me out of school. Told me to put on my coat.

"It's in the principal's office," I told him.

"Leave it, then," he said.

It was cold outside. Ice coated the trees, the rooftops of houses, the windshields of cars parked along the curbs, the sidewalks, the streets. My father drove too fast, dodging fallen tree limbs in the road, his pickup truck sliding all over, down to Pecan park. He told me to get out. Told me to open the tailgate. Told me to set the essay there on the tailgate in front of me. Told me to bend over and read each sentence, one at a time.

There was a new two-by-four in the bed of the truck. The wood was white. He picked it up, stood behind me. I read a sentence, and then he hit me one. Then I read another sentence. He hit me again. There were a hundred sentences. He kept hitting me. The wind blew up hard and it started to sleet, and all around the park tree limbs groaned and creaked and snapped off. I didn't have my coat on. I was cold. Ice fell all around me.

—first published in *Quarterly West*; 1994; reprinted in *Flash Fiction Youth*, ed. Christine Perkins-Hazuka et al.; 2011.

A teenage protagonist, yes, but a harrowing tale of topsy-turvy justice and injustice bordering on the surreal that makes this a memorable example of highly serious literary flash fiction for readers of any age. Note too how Williford's stark, truncated syntax reflects the dehumanized behavior of the teacher and the father.

Experimenting with Time

Often in flash fiction the passage of time has to be compressed, sometimes in strange ways. Backstory, for example, might present key events in the narrator's life as a series of rapid-fire sentences to give impression of lives lived out of control. I used this approach in the following story about a couple on the verge of divorcing. I wanted show the contrast between a seemingly runaway past covering many years, and a virtually paralytic present moment.

So This Is Good-Bye
by Fred D. White

This was before:

I told her I wanted nothing to do with her gossipy friends. She called me an arrogant asshole. I stopped caring about the lawn. I asked her to switch to day shift so we could do things together. "Do what?" she said. "Sit around and read books? Go out to the same god damned Chinese restaurant?" We stopped having conversations. Obscenities filled the air. Dishes shattered. Cary and Sherri slammed the front door as hard as they could on their way out of our lives. I began sleeping in one of the vacated bedrooms.

This is now:

I'm in the kitchen, checking drawers and cabinets, having finished packing up the U-Haul.

She is sitting at the kitchen table looking at her hands. "Cary and Sherri will want nothing more to do with you if you leave me."

"You're getting what you want," I say.

"I am?"

I find my corkscrew in the junk drawer and slip it into my pocket.

"You're leaving me in my old age, you bastard."

I tell her she is not in her old age.

"My knees are bad. My lower back hurts constantly."

I pour myself a glass of Kool Aid from the fridge. "Want some?"

She shakes her head. She won't stop staring at her hands.

I gulp down the Kool Aid. "I'm all set."

She stands up, goes to the sink, and stares out the window."I'll have to hire a gardener. I can't do a god damned thing with these bad knees."

I tell her I'll cover it.

"You damn well better."

I tell her that I'm going now.

"Okay. Go." She turns to face me. Her eyes are like black stones.

We continue to stand facing each other.

She presses her lips tightly together. "So this is good-bye, huh?" she says.

"Guess so."

"Well," she says, "don't let the god damn door hit you in the ass."

I continue standing there, biting my tongue so hard it makes my eyes water—just standing there as if all possibility of movement has been siphoned away.

One of the givens in any narrative is that the story moves forward in time. True, flashbacks disrupt that temporal progression, but flashbacks are always seen for what they are, and when they end the present time continues forward. One exception is the frame tale, in which the narrator presents him- or herself as the storyteller at the beginning (think of Lydgate in *Wuthering Heights*), or at the end (think of Ishmael's "Epilogue" in *Moby-Dick*, echoing the messenger in the Book of Job: "And I only am escaped alone to tell thee" (Job 1:15). But in flash fiction, you can do all sorts of things with chronology that would be difficult to sustain in longer fiction. For example, you can tell a story in reverse chronology. Consider this gem:

Currents
by Hannah Bottomy Voskuil

Gary drank single malt in the night, out on the porch that leaned toward the ocean. His mother, distracted, had shut off the floodlights and he did not protest against the dark.

Before that, his mother, Josey, tucked in her two shivering twelve-year-old granddaughters.

"I want you both to go swimming first thing tomorrow. Can't have two seals like you afraid of the water."

Before that, one of the girls held the hand of a wordless Filipino boy. His was the first hand she'd ever held. They were watching the paramedics lift the boy's dead brother into an ambulance.

At this time, the other girl heaved over a toilet in the cabana.

Before that, the girl who would feel nauseated watched as the drowned boy's hand slid off the stretcher and bounced along the porch rail. Nobody placed the hand back on the stretcher, and it bounced and dragged and bounced.

Before that, Gary saw the brown hair sink and resurface as the body bobbed. At first, he mistook it for seaweed.

Before that, thirty-five people struggled out of the water at the Coast Guard's command. A lifeguard shouted over Jet Ski motors about the increasing strength of the riptide.

Before that, the thirty-five people, including Gary and the two girls, formed a human chain and trolled the waters for the body of a Filipino boy. The boy had gone under twenty minutes earlier, and never come back up.

Before that, a lifeguard sprinted up the beach, shouting for volunteers. The two girls, resting lightly on their sandy bodyboards, stood up to help.

Before that, a Filipino boy pulled on a the torpid lifeguard's ankle and gestured desperately at the waves. My brother, he said.

Before that, it was a simple summer day.

—first published in *Quarterly West* 57 (Winter 2004); reprinted in *Flash Fiction Forward*, ed. James Thomas and Robert Shapard, Norton, 2006

Beyond just telling a story in reverse-time, Voskuil is in a sense pulling us out of time itself, thereby giving us harrowing new perspective on the blind machinations of fate.

Experimenting with Language and Style

Many flash fiction writers make use of poetic techniques like highly metaphoric or symbolic imagery, rhythm and sound, spacing and paragraphing. It is all part of the art of compression, of using traditionally poetic techniques of language and style to enhance story meaning.

Single paragraphing

By telling a story in a veritable single breath, writers create a kind of dreamlike or impressionistic mood. Let's take a look at one of my single-paragraph flash tales:

Autumn
by Fred D. White

The maitre d' seated me at a table two rows across from a woman who was sitting by herself. He handed me a leather-bound menu (one of the reasons I loved this place). Mellow jazz was playing (another reason)—it sounded like the blind George Shearing on piano, whom I had seen perform live with my ex years ago in another life. A waiter promptly approached. Would I care for a refreshing bottle of Perrier? No, thank you; tap is fine. And please bring me a vodka martini, up, with a twist, not an olive. Absolutely, sir. He bowed slightly and left. I studied the menu, even though I knew what I wanted, and looked at the woman. Except for one fleeting glance at me, she sat stone-faced, staring at the entrance. Her reddish shag-cut hair made me think of Shirley MacLaine. She was wearing a dark green silk blouse and gold earrings. I guessed her age to be mid-fifties. Any moment now, a tall man in a hand-tailored suit—someone like me twenty years ago—would appear; she would wave, and he would walk toward her, kiss her on the mouth—no, on the back of her outstretched hand, and sit down across from her. Beaming, she would lean forward to hear what he had to say. And if he were I, he'd have so much to say. The waiter returned with my martini, a glass of water, and a basket of bread. I ordered the Porterhouse, medium rare. Excellent choice, sir, our chef's specialty. He bowed again, took the menu, and darted away. The woman reached in her purse for some tissue and wiped her eyes. Suddenly our eyes met, and I looked away reflexively, wishing I hadn't done that. When I looked back, she was rummaging through her handbag again. I got up to use the restroom. Before I headed back, I combed my hair (what little was left of it) and adjusted my tie, wishing I had picked a better suit to wear. I walked past her, heart pounding, hoping she would make eye contact with me. This time, I would not look away. But she did not look up. In fact, she seemed to be making a concerted effort not to look at me. I suddenly felt as though past and present were swirling together, becoming indistinguishable. I wanted badly to say good evening to her, but she would have to look up at me first, a fleeting glance would do; but that did not happen. I returned to my table. A moment later, the maitre d' seated a couple at a table between me and the woman. I could still see her, but only partially. My hope for an autumnal romance was fading. I drank my martini, ordered another; and when the waiter returned with it, he handed me a folded slip of paper.

—first published as a podcast from *No Extra Words*,
Episode 97 (Feb., 2017). Web.

As a single paragraph, the events in the story seem to be pressed together. It's as if the narrator feels that he is running out of time—which is what I wanted to convey: he is an older man who is feeling his years, and wants very much to experience the romantic fulfillment that has always eluded him. Notice that, in addition to the title, I've inserted "autumnal" imagery—the woman's hair, her age, the fact that it is evening. Every word in a flash story should contribute to a unified impression.

Paragraphs as pigeonholes or categories

It is possible to break away from conventional narration and, borrowing from nonfiction, not so much tell a story as expose through report-like disclosures, as in the following piece by the prolific Jamaican American author, photographer, and professor (California College of the Arts, Berkeley), Opal Palmer Adisa:

Fruit Series

by Opal Palmer Adisa

Guava

The green exterior disguises perfectly the sweet pink-seeded meat that lives inside. This, her father told her, was a metaphor for how she was to dress, modestly, to hide the lascivious curves of her behind, as he was not able to protect or be with her all the time.

Breadfruit

Long ago, the god of the Taino people appeared to a guileless maiden and convinced her to allow him to sleep in her bed. The next morning she woke with a round-mounded stomach, and as she squatted in pain, the fruit spilled from her and fed the entire tribe.

Tamarind

Old age is said to be better than fortune, but she didn't agree. Left all day on the veranda, she wished she could be of use. Once, she knew which flowers were medicine and which could sweeten a pot, but now her fingers betrayed her with their stiff numbness.

Papaya

He always looked at a woman's mouth first. The shape told a lot, not just about kissing, but more, about how readily she would agree with him. Her mouth told him she was malleable; she would be good to the touch and someone worth savoring, all orange and black.

Mango

He tasted the sticky juice the moment his tongue licked her breast, and he was immediately transported to Bombay, a place he did not care to remember, where many days as a boy, all he had to eat was the fruit he stole from a tree in someone's yard.

June-Plum

Raised as he was by a mother who whipped him when frustrated, he had scars on his back and legs as proof. Still, many thought him artless to ignore such a beautiful woman who spoke gently and smiled radiantly. But he said nothing, having eaten many june-plums as a child.

Guinep

They clung to each other fiercely, vowing never to be separated, but what did they know about how time and circumstances could erode the most spirited friendship. And, after college, the distance and demands of their careers led them down different paths until the phone calls dwindled to special occasions.

Naseberry

He had been craving something sugary when he saw her in the ice cream store wearing a yellow silk dress that shimmered when she moved. He couldn't decide which flavor to order so asked her, as an opening line. She looked at him, smiled demurely, said, "Me, I'm incredibly sweet."

Otaheite Apple

Her scarlet skirt hid the purity of her heart. True, she flirted, but it was all a guise. Her innocence was fleshy white, but in his terror to possess her, to break her spirit, he bit into her, his rage covering her screams, and her ribbons fell limply.

—first published in *Zyzzyva*, Spring 2003; reprinted in *Flash Fiction Forward*, ed. James Thomas and Robert Shapard; 2006.

This strange and lovely flash tale uses many poetic elements: sensual imagery, subtle associations of fruits with aspects of romance. Still, it is very much a story, but one that is split like a rainbow into distinct spectra. As in Proust's *Remembrance of Things Past*, merely biting into a cookie can trigger a flood of memories.

Experimenting with the Intersections of Reality and Dream (Absurdist or Bizarro Flash)

This might be the point at which you start thinking that some experimental flash writers have gone off the deep end. I concede that absurd or bizarre fiction is not everyone's, or even most people's, cup of tea; but this subgenre does have the potential to show the innovative power of flash fiction (indeed, of art in general). Its predecessors include the Dada and Surrealist movements in the first half of the last century—movements that included dramatists, poets, and fiction writers, not just painters. Dramas like Samuel Beckett's *Waiting for Godot* or Eugene Ionesco's *Rhinoceros*, poems like Apollinaire's "Calligrammes," and novels like André Breton's *Nadia* together demonstrated the fertility of these complex aesthetic movements which collectively explored the interconnections between dreams and reality, and the influence of subconscious drives on communal and individual behavior as well as on modern society as a whole.

Here are a few excerpts taken from bizarre or surreal stories; think of these as *amuse-bouches* to whet your appetite for literary absurdity:

> Something was wrong with Cat Filigree. Ever since her seventeenth birthday, her skin felt tight, like someone had dipped her in glue. It slowly hardened and peeled off.
>
> —Athena Villaverde, "Caterpillar Girl"

> Years ago there was a town not far from here where nobody had their own heart. They shared one gigantic heart located in a former water purification plant near the center of town.
>
> —Ryan Boudinot, "Cardiology"

> I never had breasts until I went to Hell. When I died at the age of thirty-nine I was barely an A-cup.
>
> —Alissa Nutting, "Hellion"

> A man walked down the street with three dreams for sale.
>
> —W.S. Merwin, "A Fable of the Buyers"

Consider this bizarre flash tale by the Russian writer Daniil Kharms. Now don't be hasty in your assessment. Ask yourself just what might be the author's point, assuming he has one?

Blue Notebook No. 10
by Daniil Kharms

There was once a red-haired man who had no eyes and no ears. He also had no hair, so he was called red-haired only in a manner of speaking.

He wasn't able to talk, because he didn't have a mouth. He had no nose, either.

He didn't even have any arms or legs. He also didn't have a stomach, and he didn't have a back, and he didn't have a spine, and he also didn't have any other insides. He didn't have anything. So it's hard to understand what we're talking about.

So we'd better not talk about him anymore.

—first published in *Russia's Lost Literature of the Absurd*; translated and edited by George Gibian (Cornell UP, 1971).

So—what have you decided? Here's my take (please—don't read this until you've come to your own conclusion): Kharms is playfully describing a fictional character; and to heighten reader-awareness of that intention, he echoes that quintessential mode of storytelling, the fairy tale with the phrase, "There was once . . ."

A Note on Hybridity

Editors with increasing frequency have been calling for "hybrid works" of flash fiction. What do they mean by that? Of course, a hybrid is a mixing of properties that have originally been kept separate. In fiction writing, hybridity can mean mixing prose with poetry or prose with visuals. A hybrid fiction can even include nonfictional elements, such as photographs or charts, but put into a fictive context. A flash tale about a bootlegger in the 1920s might include a photograph of a speakeasy or a reproduction of a newspaper clipping describing a raid on one. A good example of a story using visuals this way is Donald Barthelme's "At the Tolstoy Museum," from his 1970 collection *City Life*. Here we find images of Tolstoy, examples of Tolstoy's clothes, a sketch of Tolstoy as a youth, Tolstoy with tiger hunters, etc., intermingled with the text of the story, which itself is a hybrid of weird fact and fancy ("At the Tolstoy museum we sat and wept. Paper streamers came out of our eyes . . . As a youth he [Tolstoy] shaved off his eyebrows, hoping they would grow back bushier."

Using Images as Catalysts for Flash Stories

Another way to make use of images other than interspersing them in your flash stories is to use them as catalysts. There are three ways to go about this:

1. **Enter the reality (the world) of the image**: That is, don't allude to the image as such; rather, become a participant in the scene being depicted. Take, for example, Edward Hopper's famous painting *Nighthawks*, depicting individuals in a diner in the dead of night. Your story might have your protagonist enter the diner and strike up a conversation with one of the diners or with the counterman, and, let us say, discovering through the conversation that he or she is a fugitive from the law.
2. **Create a story predicament prompted by the image**: In this case, the image reminds you of a situation you may have found yourself in, or may have imagined. Using Hopper's diner scene in *Nighthawks*, you might imagine entering a restaurant and finding a long-lost friend (or enemy)—and striking up a conversation that leads to some disturbing revelation from the past.
3. **Enter the reality (or world) of the artist:** Again using *Nighthawks* as an example, imagine a situation in which you encounter Edward Hopper, a friend, sketching a study of what will become his famous painting. What is motivating him to paint such a scene? You may want to do some research into Hopper's life beforehand.

Now It's Time to Pick Up Your Pen

1. Start working on a single-paragraph flash tale by following these steps:
   a. Brainstorm to come up with a situation that takes place in a short period of time—a half hour, say (roughly the time that elapses in "Autumn," above). The moment should have some urgency about it—a bride at the altar suddenly having second thoughts about the man she's about to marry; a disabled teen about ready to demonstrate that he can pitch a baseball as skillfully as the best of them.
   b. Write a detailed character profile of your protagonist.
   c. In one sentence, explain what is going to happen in the story, including how it will end.

d. Write a one-paragraph synopsis of the story.

e. Draft the story.

2. In the manner of Opal Palmer Odisa's "Fruit Series," write a food-related flash tale of your own. Some possibilities:
   - Moments of your narrator's childhood represented by different candies; her years in college represented by different kinds of fast food. Consider using subheads, as does Adisa, to help structure your story.
   - A prisoner represents his or her time behind bars with different prison foods.
   - Two lovers experience facets of their lives together with different dishes. (You may want to read Laura Esquivel's *Like Water for Chocolate* (subtitled *A Novel in Monthly Installments, with Recipes, Romances, and Home Remedies*) to get an idea of how a novelist handles this fusion of food with love).
3. Experiment with temporal flow in a flash story. For example, you might write a flash in which time flows differently from one character to another—or conceive of a character that moves through time in erratic ways, the way Billy Pilgrim does in Kurt Vonnegut's classic novel *Slaughterhouse-Five.*
4. Create a flash collage—one that would include, as part of the narrative, a photograph, or an excerpt from a newspaper article, or a magazine advertisement. For example, if you were to write a story about an actor who begins to develop severe stage fright, you might paste in a collage of different theater-related images (audience members' distorted faces, props, actors in costume, etc.).
5. Try your hand at composing a metafictional flash tale in which the main character becomes aware of the fact that he or she is being manipulated by you, the author, and rebels against the role you have given him or her.
6. Write a flash tale in which you blur the distinction between reality and dream. For example, have your protagonist literally bump into a person he or she had just had a dream about—and in the dream this

person had told the dreamer they would be soon be meeting "once you're awake."

7. Study one of your favorite paintings, place yourself into the world of that image, and conjure up a dramatic situation for a flash tale. Here are three paintings to consider using. (By the way, all three are reproduced in *The Story of Painting* [1994] by Sister Wendy Beckett; or you can view full-color reproductions of them on the Internet. Just Google the artist's name and title of the painting.)

    a. Pierre Renoir, *The Boating Party* (Parisians in casual dress interacting in a lively manner over lunch)

    b. Jean-Francois Millet, *The Gleaners* (peasant women in a field, gathering scraps left by the harvesters)

    c. J.M.W. Turner, *Steamboat in a Snowstorm* (a ship nearly devoured by a violent storm at sea)

Part Three

Marketing and Publishing Flash

8

Marketing and Publishing Your Flash Fiction

Now that you've been studying the art of flash fiction and have been writing (I hope!) flash tales of your own, it is time to think about getting them published. By "published" I mean accepted on a competitive basis by editors of reputable periodicals—print or online—and not self-published. There's a lot of self-publishing going on, and some of it is quite good; but in my opinion, much of it falls short of the standards set by bona fide literary journals. High standards of acceptance and keen competition lead to excellence in what makes the cut. This, I would argue, holds especially true for flash fiction.

The good news is that there are dozens of quality periodicals interested in flash fiction, several of which publish flash fiction exclusively. You should know, however, that competition is just as keen as it is with longer fiction, with acceptance rates generally between 1% and 8% . But look at competition from the bright side: you *want* your work to stand out from the crowd! I'm reminded of a *New Yorker* cartoon in which a kid comes home with a gigantic trophy, and he says to his parents, "We lost." Where is the satisfaction in getting your work accepted if the bar is set too low? Standards need to be set high or else periodicals will lose readers. Besides, high standards should inspire you to outdo yourself. One of my grad school professors used to say with regard to the then oversaturated academic job market, "There is always room at the top." The same holds true for the literary marketplace. Make up your mind to do what it takes to make it to the top. Study your craft from the inside out. Avoid scattering yourself so thin that you become the proverbial jack of all trades, master of none. Determined are you to become a top-notch flash fiction writer? Then limit yourself to flash fiction and work steadily on perfecting your craft until you reach that goal.

Building Readership

Getting your work published is half the battle these days. The other half is drumming up readers and, just as importantly, followers. Actually, you should begin publicizing your work via social media (see the following section) and email before you try to publish it in literary journals. Internet resources have somewhat blurred the boundary between publicizing and publishing; one mode of presenting your work to the public has become inextricably linked to the other.

There are several ways in which you can use Internet resources to your advantage when it comes to building readership:

1. Even before you turn to social media, look for ways to slip in a flash tale or two with a holiday or birthday greeting, especially if the theme of your story is relevant to the occasion. Do the same thing when writing letters to friends and colleagues.
2. Set up your own website. There are several website setup services available. Study each one carefully before deciding which one to go with.
3. Once your website is up, include links to every story you publish.
4. Add personal information. Readers are curious about authors—their background and family, their interests, works-in-progress, public appearances, and so on.
5. Don't expect everyone to magically become aware of your website's existence! Let friends and family know about it. Ask your writer friends to spread the word.

Using Social Media to Fine-Tune Your Flash Fiction

Like it or not, social media has become one of the most influential ways of making yourself and your work known to the general population. Connecting via Facebook, Twitter, Instagram, etc. is the twenty-first century version of inviting friends into your living room for lively conversation and (if you are all writers), manuscript sharing. The big difference of course is that your social-media "living room" encompasses the entire planet. Your virtual friends ("followers") can offer you candid and (on the most part) useful feedback on drafts of the stories you post.

Also, such draft posting will make you more audience-aware. Two thoughts on this point: First, there's a delicate balance between individual talent and reader expectation. You certainly don't want to compromise your unique manner of storytelling. At the same time, you don't want to be arrogant. "I write only for myself" is an all-too-common mantra from novice writers, and it won't serve you well. Shakespeare, the Brontë sisters, Dickens, Tolstoy, Hemingway, Steinbeck, and many other great authors all addressed a wide readership, and yet their distinctive voices and individual ways of looking at the world were never compromised. Even the most innovative writers like James Joyce, Samuel Beckett, Gertrude Stein, John Barth, Thomas Pynchon, Toni Morrison, or Haruki Murakami want their readers to experience new possibilities of literary expression.

As I pointed out elsewhere in this book, flash fiction is especially conducive to innovative and unusual approaches to storytelling; so be as eccentric as your literary heart desires. At the same time, don't forget the simple truth that writers are entertainers and enlighteners.

Here are some additional ways in which social media can help you hone your skills:

1. Initiate conversations with fellow writers on the art of fiction, on the writing process, etc. Use these conversations as a pretext for requesting feedback on a draft in progress. Of course, you'll also invite them to send *you* a draft for feedback. The more feedback you get, the better sense you will have of how to revise. Of course, some of the suggestions you'll receive simply won't ring true to your intentions.
2. Join an online writer's group. The benefits of being a regular-participating member of a writer's group are threefold: (1) you gain the discipline needed to complete projects; (2) you develop a sense of audience-awareness; (3) you strengthen your ability to master the criteria of good writing.
3. Read your flash fiction aloud to friends. Some people enjoy listening to stories more than they do reading them.

Benefitting from a Writer's Group or Workshop

Let's not forget the old fashioned and still effective way of publicizing (i.e., making public) your literary efforts: Writers' get-togethers in which works in progress are shared continue to be highly popular. Such literary get-togethers mix fun with formality in a relaxed setting (one's living room generally), with plenty of food and beverages (non-alcoholic!) on hand during breaks. They can be just as effective as their academic counterparts.

Draft sharing is an excellent way of bringing home two very important aspects of literary work: (1) Writing well is tougher than it looks, but so very rewarding when, after several revisions, a publishable story is produced; (2) You develop a keen sense of reader awareness—meaning, I hasten to add, not pandering to audience demands, but acquiring a healthy instinct for what readers crave in works of fiction. These benefits explain why even well-established writers continue to participate in their writer's groups. Members of the group are your first readers. Of course, not all of the feedback you receive will be useful to you, but the useful feedback can go a long way toward making your story publishable.

Submitting Your Work to the Flash Fiction Market

The literary marketplace today is very different from what it was in the last century, before there was an Internet, before there were electronic publications. Today there are probably more exclusively electronic journals (especially nonprofit ones, such as literary journals) than print journals, and each has its own distinctive (sometimes eccentric) literary preferences and submission requirements. A quick way to discover which periodicals publish flash fiction is to access one of the literary-journal databases on the Web. I recommend starting with the *Poets & Writers* database: <www.pw.org/literary_magazines>. Simply filter the field options by selecting "Fiction" and "Flash Fiction," clicking on any of the journals that come up, and studying their respective submission guidelines. I will list several of these markets at the end of this chapter, but keep in mind that periodicals come and go—their funding dries up, they had not gotten enough subscribers to continue operations; or the editors decide to retire or move on to more lucrative pursuits. The periodicals that do continue sometimes change their requirements, especially if new editors take over with new literary tastes and publishing agendas.

Sending your work out for consideration is serious business—your stories need to be as good as you possibly can make them to beat the competition (that is, to offer refreshingly new and powerful stories that editors haven't seen before), so resist the urge to send off your manuscript as soon as you finish it. Let it cool; that is, give yourself enough time to consider the story objectively, critically. Reread the story, blue pencil in hand, several times, even if you have been given a "go" from your social media connections and members of your writers group.

Once you think you're ready to send your work out, follow these steps:

1. Read the stories in the literary journals you want to submit to. Every editor will tell you to do this, and you may think it's just to get you to subscribe. Of course, the editors want you to subscribe, but they mean it when they say to read what they publish to get an idea of what they like. They want to see freshness, but not anything that lies outside their "aesthetic"—and sometimes their aesthetic can be rather narrow. Note that some journals publish only "themed" issues: stories submitted must reflect the theme of the upcoming issue(s).
2. Abide by the length, formatting, and other manuscript preparation requirements. Some editors will read only "blind" submissions, so you must leave off all identifying information on the manuscript, placing that information in a cover letter or in their electronic submission system instead.
3. Check the submission periods. Some journals read submissions year round, others only during specified months. For example, journals affiliated with colleges often do not solicit submissions during the summer.
4. Give your story one final proofreading. A grammatical error, misspelled word, punctuation error, or even an obvious typo may seem trivial in itself, but it signals a lack of professionalism.

Volunteering as an editor-at-large

Once you've published a flash story with a journal, volunteer your services as a "slush pile" reader for that journal. Many if not most electronic literary journals have little or no operating budget and must rely on volunteer editors and production assistants. Getting involved with the editorial side of publishing and reading through hundreds of unsolicited submissions will heighten your perception of what works and what doesn't in flash fiction writing.

Maintaining a submissions record

If you write flash fiction regularly, before long you will have accumulated a substantial body of work; and if you try marketing most of them, you'll need to maintain a careful record of what you send, where and when you send it, and when it is accepted or rejected.

Record keeping is essential if you submit your work to more than one publisher at a time. A policy of most, but definitely not all, literary journals is that you must *immediately* withdraw your submission from consideration at Journal X if Journal Y accepts it. For more about simultaneous submissions, see below.

Many periodicals require manuscripts to be submitted through Submittable, an Internet submission managing and security system. Once you are registered with Submittable, you simply submit your work through a member journal's Submittable submission page. Through Submittable, it is possible to withdraw a work from one journal (either because you've decided to revise it or because it was accepted by another journal). It is also possible to submit revisions via Submittable, but only if the editor requests them.

Editorial reporting times

Editors of literary journals most likely have day jobs; moreover, even obscure journals receive a great many submissions, hundreds each week, and so reporting times can take quite a while—sometimes as long as eight months. Fortunately, most editors will respond within three months, and a few will report within a week. Once you submit a story, turn your attention to working on another story.

Simultaneous submissions

In pre-Internet days, sending a manuscript to more than one publisher at a time was frowned upon; but thanks to email and electronic submission systems, most publishers accept simultaneous submissions, *provided that you contact them immediately if the piece is accepted elsewhere.* I certainly recommend this practice if the periodical(s) in question have reporting times of more than three months.

Reading fees

To stay solvent, many journals charge a modest reading fee (usually three or five dollars). Some of these fee-charging journals are prestigious; some even pay their contributors (imagine!). I am all for supporting these journals via reading fees—and by subscribing to them, too. We writers need to support the literary arts in any way we can.

A word about payment: Most of the time, the pay, if any, is tokenistic, sometimes known euphemistically as an honorarium. Whenever I am offered payment for a flash tale (usually somewhere between ten and twenty dollars), I donate it back to the magazine. Look: the real payment comes from exposure, the possibility that it will be selected for a prize or an anthology.

A list of periodicals that feature flash fiction

Note that this is a partial and possibly ephemeral listing. Before you submit your work to these periodicals, be sure to check their respective websites for their latest editorial needs and length requirements, as well as to check if they're still in business. Literary journals sometimes, alas, fold because of lack of subscribers or other sources of funding.

2 Elizabeths
3 A.M
365 Tomorrows [science fiction]
Agni
All the Sins
A-Minor Magazine
Analog [humorous/satirical science fiction]
Apricity Press
Apt
Ariel Chart
Arkana
The Arcanist [fantasy, science fiction]
Arts & Letters
Atticus Review
Bartleby Snopes
Bayou Magazine
Beautiful Losers
Beloit Fiction Journal
Black Heart Magazine
Blue Earth Review
Blue Monday
The Boiler Journal
Brilliant Flash Fiction
Burningword Literary Journal
Cactus Heart
Café Irreal
Cease, Cows
Clockwise Cat [mostly satirical and humorous flash]
Cobalt
The Collagist
Concis
The Courtship of Winds

Crack the Spine
Daily Science Fiction
Delmarva Review
The Doctor T.J. Eckleburg Review
The Ekphrastic Review [fiction inspired by works of art]
Eleven Eleven
Empyreome [science fiction and fantasy]
Fiction Southeast
Five Points
Flash: The International Short-Short Story Magazine
Flash Fiction Magazine
Flash Fiction Online
Freeze Frame Fiction
Funny in Five Hundred [humorous and satirical flash]
Every Day Fiction
Freeze Frame Fiction
Gemini Magazine
Ginosko Literary Journal
Gone Lawn
Gravel
Gulf Coast
The Higgs Weldon
The Hungry Chimera
Inch
The Journal Magazine
Journal of Compressed Creative Arts
Lascaux Review
Lipstick Party
Literary Juice
Literary Orphans
Madhat Lit
Madcap Review
Mithila Review [speculative science fiction/fantasy only]
Molotov Cocktail
Monkeybicycle
Mortar Magazine
Nanoism [Twitter fiction only]
Olentangy Review
Pacifica Literary Review

Pank
Paper Darts
Pidgeonholes
Pleiades
Praxis Literary Journal
Print-Oriented Bastards
Quarter After Eight
Quarterly West
Rathalla Review
Riggwelter
Rivet
Satire and More
Smokelong Quarterly
Spilled Milk
Steel Toe Magazine
Stoneslide Corrective
Storm Cellar
Subtropics
Tahoma Literary Review
Tin House
Tishman Review
Vestal Review
West Texas Literary Review
Whiskey Island
Wigleaf
Willow Springs
The Writing Disorder

Writing the cover letter

Cover letters are more important for story collections (see Chapter 9) than for submission of individual flash tales; but most literary journals nevertheless appreciate a brief cover letter introducing yourself and your writing projects, along with a recent publishing history. Because most work is submitted online rather than via snail mail, a cover letter box is included in the journal's submission system.

Flash Fiction Contests

Several literary journals host flash fiction competitions, so it is worthwhile to enter them. The competition is fierce, though, so you'll want to make sure the stories you enter are top-notch. Expect to pay a reading fee of usually $10–$20 for a single story.

Here are some of the literary journals that sponsor an annual or biannual flash fiction competition. Be sure to check the websites for guidelines and deadlines, as they sometimes are updated.

- *American Short Fiction*/American Short[er] Fiction Prize
  www.americanshortfiction.org
- *Field of Words Flash Fiction Competition*
  www.fieldofwords.com.au
- *Fiction Southeast*/Ernest Hemingway Flash Fiction Prize
  www.fictionsoutheast.com
- Fish Publishing/Flash Fiction Prize
  www.fishpublishing.com
- *Gemini Magazine*
  www.gemini-magazine.com
- *Glimmer Train*/Very Short Fiction Award
  www.glimmertrain.com
- *Gulf Coast*/Barthelme Prize
  www.gulfcoastmag.org
- *Midway Journal*
  www.midwayjournal.com
- *Quarter After Eight*/Robert J. Demott Short Prose Contest
  www.quarteraftereight.org

For suggestions on preparing a flash fiction collection for competitions, see Chapter 9.

Now It's Time to Pick Up Your Pen

1. Submit a flash story to a literary journal:
   a. Study the submission guidelines for several literary journals (Google their titles or locate a literary journals database to access journal websites). Access the journal's archives to read what they have published. Select a journal that seems a close fit for your work. Before you send your flash fiction to them, revise and proofread your work one last time.

b. Write a succinct cover letter. Be sure to state whether your submission is a simultaneous one or an exclusive one. Also assure the editor that the work you're sending them has not been published before. Many literary journals specify the kinds of flash fiction they like to publish. Write a story that precisely meets the criteria for one of these journals.

2. Select three of your flash stories and submit them to your writers group (or to a friend whose objectivity and candor you trust). Before you share them, make sure they're as good as you can make them. After receiving feedback, revise accordingly and submit them to one or more literary journals. Select three of your flash stories and submit them to your writers group (or to a friend whose objectivity and candor you trust). Before you share them, make sure they're as good as you can make them. After receiving feedback, revise accordingly and submit them to one or more literary journals.

3. Get to work on a flash tale that meets one or more of the criteria set forth in the guidelines of a literary journal. After you draft the story, access that journal's archives to read some of the stories they published, and to compare it with your draft. If you get the sense that your story needs to be revised, revise it; if you think it's as good or better than the stories they published, send it in.

4. Dig out a flash story from your "needs more work" folder and revise it in accordance with the guidelines of a literary journal whose published fiction you have read and admired. After carefully studying those stories for structure, characterization, setting, descriptive power, and voice, rework your own story in a way that would please the editor(s), and submit it to them.

9

Preparing a Volume of Flash Fiction

The best way to set yourself up for stardom (okay, for recognition) as a writer of flash tales is to win a contest, the major prize for which (besides a cash award) is having a collection of *your* stories assembled into a chapbook (usually 20-40 pages). On occasion, some publishers or organizations will sponsor competitions or "open readings" for full-length story collections (150-250 pages). Typically, such full-length collections will include short stories of conventional length (2000-7000 words), with perhaps an occasional flash tale or two. Yes, there are sometimes competitions for exclusively flash fiction collections, but they are not as common.

Because book publishers and agents, with very few exceptions, do not consider full-length story collections from unknown authors, chapbook competitions are one of the best ways to get noticed. Competition is fierce; the larger the prize, the larger the number of entries. Expect to pay a fee of $15–$30 for each manuscript you enter; and yes, most contests will allow you to submit as many entries as you wish, each with its own entry fee, of course. Several fiction chapbook competitions are announced annually, so check the online databases frequently for announcements.

This chapter offers pointers on how to make your chapbook collection of flash tales stand out among the hundreds (sometimes thousands) of entries that any given competition will attract. Before you consider assembling a chapbook, though, be sure that each of your completed flash tales is polished and error-free. Also, you ought to have many more finished stories than you need for a collection, so that you are able to select the crème de la crème from your repertoire. Let's go over the basic guidelines.

Basic Guidelines for Success in Competitions

The following suggestions apply to any competition you enter. Of course, individual sponsors will have their own specific guidelines.

1. Study the guidelines for each competition carefully and prepare your manuscript exactly as instructed. If the guidelines express openness to all themes and styles, take that with a grain of salt and study the past winners. The competition sponsor may prefer realism over experimental modes, or vice versa. If the guidelines state that entries are read blindly, then make sure no identifying information appears anywhere on the manuscript. If you overlook that rule, your entry could be automatically disqualified.

2. Find out who the judge is and read his or her published work. This is not to suggest that the judge will be biased toward selecting a winning entry that comes closest to his or her own preferences in flash fiction, but it could nonetheless hint at particular predilections. If the judge's own stories are filled with grittily realistic portraits of life in urban jungles, you may want to shelve your stories about mermaids and flying horses and instead prepare a volume that at least features characters in challenging environments (not necessarily urban). Of course, there is always the option of entering your collection of fantasy or bizarro flash in another contest.

3. Ensure that each story is as good as it possibly can be. If you have any lingering doubts about a story, it most likely needs to be rewritten. Rewrite it until you are *completely* satisfied with it; otherwise, exclude it from the manuscript. A weak or flawed story casts a pall over the entire collection.

4. Read the entries of previous chapbook competition winners—not just read but study carefully, paying close attention to technique. This is a crucial step. You want to gain a full appreciation of what it takes for judges to decide that the stories in a particular manuscript outshined a thousand others.

5. Proofread! Errors in grammar, spelling, and punctuation may seem superficial relative to story content, but the harsh fact is that such blemishes convey unprofessionalism and will reduce your chances of making it through the first round of screenings. Revisions are not accepted during the judging period unless the manuscript is selected

as a winner. At best you would have to withdraw the manuscript and resubmit it with a new entry fee.

How to Give Your Book or Chapbook the Competitive Edge

There are seven things to consider when preparing a chapbook of flash fiction for a competition:

1. Accumulate a sufficiently large pool of finished material to choose from.
2. Try publishing your stories in literary journals first.
3. Arrange stories around common themes, motifs, or settings.
4. Use aesthetic criteria for sequencing the stories.
5. Give your stories intriguing titles.
6. Select striking or representative stories for the first and last slots.
7. Use the title of the most representative story for the title of the collection.

Accumulate a sufficiently large pool of finished material to choose from

The biggest mistake writers make when entering a literary competition is that they include work recently finished—typically within the preceding week. The problem is that they don't yet have an objective perspective on the work. They often feel it is their best work yet, and it just might be; but more often than not, it is just the afterglow of completing a story. I too have succumbed to afterglow and entered a chapbook that included stories I had completed during the preceding couple of weeks . . . only to realize several days later that I overlooked significant matters of structure and language. True, easier said than done, but don't be hasty when it comes to submitting your work. Believe me, you will save yourself a lot of time and frustration in the long run.

If you are preparing a chapbook, select as many stories as needed to fill between 24 and 40 manuscript pages, not including front matter or an acknowledgments page. (Different chapbook publishers have somewhat different length requirements.) If you are preparing a full-length collection, the minimum is 48 pages and the norm is roughly 150-200 pages.

Try publishing your stories in literary journals first

Although not a criterion for judging, journal publication of your stories at least lets you know that the stories have not only survived editorial "slush piles," but passed muster during final editorial screening as well If any of your stories have been rejected by several editors, they should be thoroughly revised. I do not, however, recommend discarding stories just because they've been rejected. It may take you a few more months, maybe even years, before you're able to figure out how to improve them.

Arrange stories around common themes, motifs, or settings

Stories in a chapbook sometimes are grouped around one or more themes (whether stated explicitly or not), such as "forgiveness" or "loss of innocence"; or motifs such as stories involving computers, or stories about interacting with wild animals.

Many writers arrange their stories according to setting. Sherwood Anderson's most famous book is his collection of stories all set in a fictional small town: *Winesburg, Ohio*. The town itself emerges as a veritable character in the collection. Similarly, John Updike published dozens of stories set in the fictional town of Olinger, Pennsylvania, later collected as *Olinger Stories*.

If your stories are linked—that is, taken together, they can be read as a coherent whole (like the stories in Ernest Hemingway's *In Our Time* or in William Faulkner's *Go Down, Moses*)—then it might make sense to arrange them in chronological order. But that is not a necessity.

Use aesthetic criteria for sequencing the stories

Another way to arrange your flash tales in a collection is to use aesthetic criteria. Basically, you ask yourself which stories resonate best when placed next to each other. For example, a dark and brooding story will seem even darker and more brooding if it follows a witty or whimsical one. A stylistically innovative story may be appreciated more if it follows a more conventional one. Other aesthetic criteria include:

- Variations in length (say a 1000-word story followed by a 500-word story)
- Contrasting personalities or ages of the respective protagonists
- Non-sequential chronology (e.g., one story set in the narrator's old age, followed by another set in his or her childhood, followed by another set during adolescence)

- Contrasting story types (e.g., a literary flash followed by a genre flash)
- Contrasting story moods (e.g., a sad or dark story followed by a lively one)

Give your stories intriguing titles

So what constitutes an intriguing title? Anything that sparks curiosity. It can include word-play, the term for the narrator's state of mind, the story's central incident, or an object in the story that resonates symbolically.

Select striking or representative stories for the first and last slots

Imagine a customer in a bookstore flipping through your book, trying to decide whether to purchase it or not. She starts reading the first story; will it grab her attention? Of course, there are other criteria for choosing the opening story: does it set the tone for the entire collection? Does it introduce one of your most complex characters, the one whose complexity will be most appreciated after the subsequent stories are read?

As for the concluding story: like the concluding movement of a symphony, it should leave readers with a sense of completion, not unlike the concluding scene of a novel or of a motion picture.

Use the title of the most representative story for the title of the collection

The "most representative" story would be the story with a theme that recurs in some manner in most or all of the other stories. This is not a hard rule. You might choose a title that describes the setting (if all the stories are set in one location), or alludes to the situations in the stories (e.g., "Haunted Hotel" if all of the stories take place in such a place). Criteria for selecting the title of a story collection are more aesthetic than logical. Although titles cannot be copyrighted, it is prudent to ensure that the title you choose has not been used before—or at least has not been used recently. Hint: Go to the Library of Congress website, www.loc.gov, and enter your title into their search engine.

Writing a Query Letter

Occasionally for open-reading solicitations, the editor will ask you to submit a query letter first in which you describe your story collection. The effectiveness or ineffectiveness of your letter, and whether your project seems to be a good fit their publishing program, or not, will determine whether the editor asks you to send along the manuscript. To increase your chances of getting a reading, be sure your query letter includes the following:

- A clear, well-detailed overview of the collection: the kinds of stories, their principal themes or motifs or settings, the total number of stories.
- A list of where the stories were previously published. If you have not published any of the stories, that is not usually a detriment; editors are concerned with the quality of the stories and their potential appeal.
- A brief autobiography, focusing on your experiences insofar as they connect to the stories, your presence on social media, your website if you have one.

Writing a Cover Letter

First impressions matter when submitting your manuscript for consideration. A cover letter should introduce your book in a way that arouses the editor's or contest judge's curiosity about the collected stories. But be careful: avoid superlatives or other forms of advertising rhetoric. As in a query letter, a cover letter should include:

- An overview of the collection: how the stories interconnect (if at all), the predominant themes or motifs, the principal settings.
- A summary of the stories' publication history (in addition to an Acknowledgments page in the manuscript itself).
- A brief biographical statement, including experiences that relate directly or indirectly to the stories themselves. For example, if your stories are set in war zones and you have experience as, say, an overseas correspondent or served in the military, be sure to mention that.

What about Prize Money or Royalties?

If you win a chapbook competition, you will most likely receive a cash award of anywhere from $100 to $1000.00. Sometimes there will not be a cash award at all, but that shouldn't discourage you: a published chapbook can get you recognized by editors, maybe even literary agents.

If you win first prize for a book-length collection, you will most likely receive a cash award, usually between $1000 and $2000 (which could double as an advance against royalties), and a standard book contract, with royalties payable once or twice a year. Winning such a prize can bring you widespread recognition as a fiction writer. Literary agents keep an eye out for book prize winners.

Occasionally, small book publishers will hold "open readings" for a limited time (usually a month), during which time they will consider unagented story collections. If your flash fiction collection is accepted, you will probably not receive an advance, but will receive royalties.

Here are some of the annual short fiction competitions for chapbook or book-length collections (check the websites for guidelines and deadlines):

- Autumn House Press/Fiction Prize www.autumnhouse.org
- Black Lawrence Press/Hudson Prize/St. Lawrence Book Awards www.blacklawrence.com
- BOA Editions/Short Fiction Prize boaeditions.org
- *Cutbank*/Chapbook Contest www.cutbankonline.org
- Elixir Press/Fiction Award www.elixirpress.com
- Engine Books/Fiction Prize www.enginebooks.org
- *Florida Review*/Jeanne Leiby Memorial Chapbook Award www.floridareview.cah.ucf.edu
- Leapfrog Press/Fiction Award www.leapfrogpress.com
- Livingston Press/Tartt Fiction Award. www.livingstonpress.uwa.edu
- Mad River Books/Journal Fiction Collection Prize www.thejournalmag.org
- Omnidawn Fabulist Fiction Chapbook Contest ww.omnidawn.com
- *Pleiades Press*/Robert C. Jones Prize for Short Prose www.pleiadespress.org
- Press 53/Award for Short Fiction

Now It's Time to Pick Up Your Pen

1. Organize a volume of your work:
    a. Gather all of the flash stories you've written—all of them, including the ones you've given up on and the ones you haven't finished. (By the way, I advise you never to discard a story, no matter how bad you think it is, or how unlikely you'll ever finish it; you can never

tell what spark of insight might make it work.) I recommend printing out all of this material if they're all on computer files.

b. If you're planning a chapbook, select as many stories as will fill forty pages. Begin each story on a new page.

c. Using the suggestions I've given you in this chapter, arrange the stories in some kind of logical or aesthetic sequence.

2. Write a query letter in which you pitch your story collection to a book publisher.

3. Write a cover letter for your chapbook. When writing the paragraph that describes the stories, pretend that you are writing the jacket copy for your book.

4. Outline a chapbook of flash fiction in which every story features the same protagonist and perhaps one or two other characters. Build the stories around a central theme, such as the difficulties of reconciliation (friends or family or both). Before working on the stories themselves, prepare profile sheets for each character (see Chapter 5 for suggestions).

5. Write a one-sentence premise for each flash tale you intend to include in your chapbook. If these any of these sentences do not seem compelling, re-examine the stories and revise them until their premises do seem compelling.

6. Expand your premise sentences into one-paragraph synopses. As with the premise sentences, make sure that each synopsis is compelling; otherwise revise the story.

7. Spend a generous amount of time drafting each story; don't settle for the first things that come to mind, even though there's something to be said for spontaneity. Once you've completed the ten or twelve stories needed for the chapbook, read them aloud to friends or fellow workshop participants. Take notes on suggested revisions but do not revise them yet; instead, let the stories "percolate" in your subconscious for a few days. Finally, revise each story, but carefully, methodically, over a period of several days. Hastiness will likely work against you.

10

Concluding Reflections and a Self-Interview

"The arts are not algebra," the nineteenth century French romantic painter Eugene Delacroix wrote in his journal. He meant that you cannot reduce art to any formula because the desire to make art stems from the need to *enlarge* our deeply felt experience of the world, not reduce it. Delacroix adds, pointedly, "Success in the arts is by no means a matter of abridging but of amplifying."* Although flash stories might seem like abridgements or synopses because of their extreme brevity, there is indeed amplification—not in the conventional manner of a novel or even of traditional-length short stories (1000–7000 words), but by way of the techniques of indirection, allusion, and innuendo described earlier. "Good one-page fictions," states the novelist and flash fiction writer Jayne Anne Phillips, in an essay titled "'Cheers,' (or) How I Taught Myself to Write," "have a spiral construction: the words circle out from a dense, packed core, and the spiral moves through the words, past the boundary of the page." Phillips goes on to say, "I taught myself to write by writing one-page fictions."

Flash and the World of Story

Fiction of any length can pull you into the world of the story so you can experience its reality vicariously; but flash fiction only offers you enough time for a fleeting glimpse (think of casting a flashlight beam onto a scene full of activity)—or to change sensory metaphors, a tantalizing taste of its world, and pulls you away before you can take another bite. Done effectively, that quick dip is enough to leave you with a powerful impression. It makes you want to come back for more. Of course, you can always re-enter the story world you conjured up in a flash tale—over and over,

*Quoted by Simon O. Lesser, *Fiction and the Unconscious* (1962).

each time capturing another facet of that world by reading another flash piece. These separate pieces can stand on their own; at the same time, collectively, they may result in a flash fiction novel. Think, for example, of Ernest Hemingway's linked stories comprising *In Our Time*, Sherwood Anderson's *Winesburg, Ohio*, F. Scott Fitzgerald's *The Pat Hobby Stories*, or Annie Proux's beautifully illustrated *Close Range: Wyoming Stories*.

Flash Fiction and the Literary Life

There's something fundamental to the literary life about flash fiction writing, in that flash fiction helps train a writer to use language to capture the essence of a situation. Flash fiction also serves as basic training for any other kind of writing.

Flash fiction, for me, represents a unique kind of literary free-play. Because of its brevity, you can create well-made literary and genre flash tales using the guidelines I've provided; but you can also shelve the methodologies and write without restraint—write to give free reign to the play-drive all human beings possess but do not know how to exploit to fullest creative advantage. Play pulls us out of our rational (often over-rational) selves and gives us the courage to think and act differently, and that includes new ways of expressing reality with language. In *Homo Ludens*, a seminal study on the role of play in culture and in human behavior, the Dutch scholar Johan Huizinga points out that poetry (and by implication all art, including flash fiction) is "born in play." From the perspective of play, even an individual word "is a small story," as the poet-essayist Diane Ackerman wrote in her book, *Deep Play*. Moreover, to quote Ackerman again, "to play is to risk: to risk is to play." I would also point out that risk-taking is essential to creativity (itself a fundamental aspect of play); and, at least for me, flash fiction is the ideal medium for learning to become a creative risk-taker.

Writing flash fiction not only heightens your play-drive, it can make you prolific. When I turned to flash fiction several years ago, my output increased tenfold. For a while I was drafting a story idea nearly every day. Never mind that many of these stories turned out to be duds; every story I worked on enhanced my desire to write more. The more I wrote flash, the more I wanted to write.

On a Personal Note

What drew me originally to flash fiction, both as a reader and a writer (and I'll say more about this in my self-interview, below), was its affinity with poetry. A good poem captures a facet of experience conventional prose cannot, and does so with highly metaphoric, compressed language. Emily Dickinson compared poetic compression to the attar of roses, calling such compression "the gift of Screws." Flash fiction has that kind of poetic compression. By the way, I strongly recommend that writers of flash fiction study the poetry of Emily Dickinson; she is the preeminent master of compression.

Flash fiction, like lyric poetry, comes closest to communicating what words cannot express, or what it would take a great many words to express. Flash fiction, I discovered, manages to tell a story, or pull us into a fictive moment, and generate complex emotions at the same time.

Self-Interview

Q. What fascinates you about flash fiction, as a reader of flash and as a writer of flash?

A. Flash fiction has the capacity to conjure up mysterious and even magical aspects of experience, not just with its use of language, but with its storytelling techniques. Through sparse, often unconventional narrative voices, good flash fiction imparts a *flash* of insight into the human condition. The flash—the suddenness of the moment—is important. Like a flash of lightning, it simultaneously illuminates and spooks a landscape. Not surprisingly, many writers of flash are also poets. I'd go so far as to say that writing flash is like composing both poetry and fiction at the same time. However, while a flash tale is compressed like a poem (deploying many techniques typically associated with poetry such as symbolism, metaphor, sensory imagery), it differs from a poem in that it typically pays little or no attention to rhythm and meter, and major attention to story and characters.

Q. Can you say more about the compression factor in flash fiction?

A. Aside from the compression techniques that I discuss throughout the book, I would argue that compression is an elusive art. A good flash writer brings elements into a story that resonate; that is to say, one set of story elements (for example, activities or descriptions of persons) may illuminate other elements of the story. A description of a dilapidated house, for example, may not only correspond to a character's disheveled appearance, but also imply a causal connection—that the character was somehow *responsible* for the house's deterioration. A story depicting temperamental passengers on a cruise ship might resonate effectively with unpredictable ocean weather.

I am also fascinated by the kinds of compression flash writers can create through masterful use of syntax and sentence structure. A skillfully constructed sentence embeds information with optimum efficiency by using a medley of syntactic devices, like parallel construction ("Judge people not by the color of their skin but by the content of their character."); independent clauses ("We skipped the party but we attended the concert."); subordinate clauses ("Because we attended the concert, we skipped the party."); parenthetical phrases (like this); and several other devices. In 2004 I published in the literary journal *Pleiades* an essay titled simply "Sentences," on the verbal magic and music sentences can conjure up. "Writers of all stripes, from aspiring poets to students in first-year composition courses," I argue in that essay, "should become riverboat pilots of syntax, urged to do their own steering, however frightful it may be for them initially." That is to say, mastering the possibilities of syntax is one of the most effective ways to make your writing distinctive.

Q. Should flash writers plan "resonances" beforehand?

A. They can try! Sometimes these resonances are thought out beforehand; other times it is sheer serendipity at work: things magically come together in lovely synchronicity because the writer's mind is fully engaged with the story world.

Writers of flash fiction should regularly practice compressing not only their stories in progress, but their older stories. Try shrinking them to half their original length while still retaining the story's essential premise. "Taylor's States," one of the flash tales of mine included in this book (Chapter 5), was originally twice as long. It's surprising how the compression enhances the story elements, makes the story more readable, more intense.

Q. Some say that flash fiction has become popular because readers today have shorter attention spans, or have less time for leisurely reading. Do you buy either of those reasons?

A. No. That would be like saying readers of poetry have shorter attention spans than readers of novels. It really is not an either-or issue; many readers of flash, myself included, read novels just as avidly. This leads me to make a point about flash fiction I cannot overemphasize: although flash fiction tends to be defined mainly by length, *compressed story*, not length, is its most salient feature.

Q. What inspired you to write a book about writing flash fiction?

A. Well, I'm a teacher, now retired (professor emeritus, Santa Clara University), as well as a writer, and I can never resist the urge to combine one with the other. In fact, as I used to tell my students, writing is itself a form of teaching. Writing is for me as tough a skill to master as teaching; and once I learned to write with some competence, I wanted to teach others to write well. Writing well goes hand in hand with thinking well. I was convinced that with proper guidance, the obstacles are easier—or at least less difficult—to overcome, and the apprentice years I just alluded to can be whittled down a bit. I like to think that, with my forty-plus years of teaching writing, and publishing dozens of flash stories, that I can help student writers leap over the hurdles. Learning to write flash fiction is an excellent way to become adept at all other kinds of writing.

Q. Who are your favorite flash fiction writers?

A. Besides myself? Just kidding—okay, not entirely; you have to believe in yourself, in your ability to outshine other writers, or else you'll sink under the weight of competition. Look, every writer has a unique way of seeing the world, and the challenge is to find ways to capture that uniqueness in language. So, to answer the question: among the trailblazers there's Kafka, Hemingway, Raymond Carver, Richard Brautigan, Henry Slesar, Fredric Brown, Arthur C. Clarke (the last three being science fiction writers; see *Microcosmic Tales* in the For Further Reading section). Among contemporary flash writers, there's Ben Loory, Bruce Holland Rogers, Joy Williams, Opal Palmer Adisa—

Q. Who coined the term *flash fiction*, by the way?

A. James Thomas, one of the groundbreaking anthologists. I've listed his (and his co-editor's) anthologies under For Further Reading. But flash fiction existed long before Thomas coined the term (in 1992, I believe). See Chapter 1 for my summary of the roots of the genre.

Q. I interrupted you. Who are some other favorite flash fiction writers of yours?

A. Let's see . . . Italo Calvino—his *Invisible Cities* is a good example of how you can build self-contained flash tales around a basic theme or motif;

Amy Hempel; Stuart Dybek (also a widely published poet—no surprise); Lydia Davis—a master of short fiction. Her *Collected Stories* (most of which are flash tales) won one of the most prestigious prizes in literature, the Man Booker Prize. By the way, Davis has extended flash fiction to include single-paragraph, even single-sentence, mystical (and sometimes baffling) nuggets. I keep coming across gifted flash writers whose work appears in the many online literary journals.

Q. Is it true that some periodicals publish flash fiction as podcasts?

A. Yes. One of my flash tales, "Autumn" (which appears in Chapter 7), has been published as a podcast by *No Extra Words.* According to James Thomas, et al., in their Introduction to *Flash Fiction International*, flash fiction has been read to audiences on Broadway, and those readings subsequently broadcast on National Public Radio.

Q. What common mistakes do beginning flash fiction writers make?

A. The same mistakes most writers make: not enough in-depth study of the art of the flash tale; not enough diligence when it comes to practicing the craft. It's important to commit to an apprenticeship stage, when their initial efforts will most likely not get past the circular file. This book will serve as a guide through that apprenticeship. Impatience with getting into print is another mistake. Ray Bradbury said he had to write *one hundred* stories before he finally got the hang of it. So: be patient and diligent. Write every day; revise, revise, revise! And share your work (third or fourth draft, never your first) with others—but not your spouse, unless you're certain he or she can be objective, even ruthless.

Q. What is the best way to become prolific at flash fiction writing?

A. Flash fiction, like poetry, is easy to write badly, so if you knock off a flash tale or two every day, you will soon have a pile of stories, but they may well be junk. To write quality fiction of any length takes time and deep concentration. A flash tale worthy of publication—and posterity—may take you several weeks' worth of revisions to perfect. Strive then to become a quality writer, not a prolific one.

Q. I can't name any famous flash fiction writers the way I can name famous novelists. How come?

A. Give it time. Flash fiction is still a relatively new mode of storytelling. I have a hunch that single-author flash-fiction collection best-sellers will appear in the near future.

Q. So you're saying that flash fiction has a future, and is not just a passing fad?

A. Flash is here to stay! It has become a global phenomenon. There are even national flash fiction day celebrations in Great Britain and New Zealand. The many anthologies and periodicals devoted to it, the contests, tell me that flash fiction will not only prevail but thrive, mainly because it is so open to innovation.

Q. Thanks for taking the time to talk with me.

A. You're quite welcome.

Now It's Time to Pick Up Your Pen

What, you thought you were through doing exercises just because this is the concluding chapter?

1. Spend a full hour writing in the spirit of play. Don't brainstorm for a story, just free-associate, letting whatever words and phrases that pop into your head take you places you had not anticipated. You might start with a single word, pulled at random out of a dictionary—or an image from a collection of paintings or photographs.
2. Write a self-interview in which you explain to yourself what you find most interesting about flash fiction and the writing of it, based on what you have learned from this book
3. Get to work on a flash story that will represent your very best flash fiction writing skills. Brainstorm to come up with a strong subject and premise. After writing a first draft, let it sit for a while, and then revise it. Read it aloud and/or have it critiqued by more than one person. Revise it again, based on the feedback you receive.
4. Plan a trio of interconnected flash stories based on three phases of your protagonist's life (childhood-adolescence-adulthood would be an obvious trio; but also consider phases based on three momentous activities, three life-changing revelations, three romances, three countries visited).

   First, take notes (or brainstorm) for each of the three events; next, write out a one-sentence description for each phase, making sure you add transitional sentences to link the three phases together; next, expand each sentence into a paragraph synopsis; and finally, draft the stories.

5. Practice story compression by writing a 250-word flash tale in which a circus clown convinces a child that the circus is the real world.
6. Take the flash tale you wrote for #5 and reduce it to 100 words.
7. Dig out some of your longer stories and rewrite them as flash tales. The best way to go about this task is first to determine the gist of each story, its essence. Write it out in one or two sentences. Now add to those sentences only what is crucial to its story-ness.

A Flash Fiction Checklist

Refer to this checklist frequently while composing a flash story, and especially before submitting your work to publishers.

_____Do I have a compelling idea for a flash tale?

_____Have I prepared a detailed character profile for each of my characters, including the narrator?

_____Is there a *story*, even though much of it is implied?

  _____Is the situation quickly established?

  _____Is the setting clear?

  _____Is there some complication, conflict, or obstacle preventing the protagonist from achieving his or her objective?

  _____Have I presented the climactic moment or epiphany effectively?

_____Are the characters sufficiently delineated for a flash tale?

_____Can I describe what the story is about in a single sentence?

_____Does the narrative progress in a coherent manner?

_____Have I described the setting (exterior, interior) in enough detail for the reader to visualize it clearly?

_____Are my descriptions vivid and specific?

_____Does every word, sentence, and paragraph contribute to the whole?

_____Is there anything I can cut without diminishing the story, and might even strengthen the story? In flash fiction less is often more!

_____Does the opening sentence grab attention, arouse curiosity?

_____Does the last sentence give the story a sense of an ending (if not necessarily a logical conclusion)?

_____Does the story feel complete even if it presents a quick glimpse into a situation?

_____Is the story readable? That is, are the sentences tightly written, well-constructed, able to invoke the desired atmosphere?

_____Have I chosen the precise words and phrasing to capture the desired emotional effect?

_____Have I avoided trite or stale words and expressions?

_____Did I give the story an intriguing title?

_____Did I proofread my story carefully for errors in usage, misspellings, awkward phrasing?

References

Stories Appearing in this Book

Adisa, Opal Palmer. "Fruit Series." *ZYZZYVA*, Spring 2003.

Aesop, "The Farmer and the Stork." *Aesop's Fables.*

Anonymous, "The Executive and the Witch," *Playboy* Magazine, March 1964; reprinted in Norman N. Holland, *The Dynamics of Literary Response.* New York: Oxford U.P., 1968.

Cherches, Peter, "Double Date." *North American Review*; reprinted in *Flash Fiction Funny*, ed. Tom Hazuka. San Francisco: Blue Light Press/1st World Publishing, 2013.

Faith, Utahna. "All-Girl Band." *Café Irreal* #3; reprinted in *Flash Fiction Forward*, ed. James Thomas and Robert Shapard. New York:W.W. Norton & Co., 2006.

Flick, Sherrie, "7:23 P.M." From *I Call This Flirting.* Chico, CA: Flume Press, 2004.

Jancewicz, Anna Lea. "Marriage." matchbook lit mag, Aug. 2014; reprinted in *The Best Small Fictions 2015*, ed. Robert Olen Butler. Plano, TX: Queen's Ferry Press, 2015.

Kharms, Daniil, "Blue Notebook No. 10." In *Russia's Lost Literature of the Absurd.* Trans. George Gibian. Cornell: Cornell University Press, 1971. Reprinted in *Imperial Messages*, ed. Howard Schwartz. New York: Avon Books, 1976.

Negroni, Maria. "The Baby." Translated by Anne Twitty. From *Night Journey.* Princeton: Princeton University Press, 2002. Reprinted in *Flash Fiction International.*

Nelson, Antonya, "Land's End." *Microfiction: An Anthology of Really Short Stories*, ed. Jerome Stern. New York: W.W. Norton & Co., 1996.

Voskuil, Hannah Bottomy, "Currents." *Quarterly West 57* (Winter 2004). Reprinted in *Flash Fiction Forward*, ed. James Thomas and Robert Shapard. New York: W.W. Norton & Co., 2006.

White, Fred D. "Autumn." *No Extra Words*. Podcast; Episode 97; Feb. 2017.

———, "Black Lives Matter."

———, "Brainies." *Every Day Fiction*. March 2017. Web.

——— "Bremer in Extremis," *Praxis Literary Journal*, May15, 2016. Web.

——— "The Bully."

———, "A Community Reckoning."

———, "The Confession." *Burningword* Literary Journal. Web.

———, "The Face in the Rock." *Aphelion*. May, 2016. Web.

———, "A Horoscope for the Astronomically Minded. *Clockwise Cat* #38; Sept. 2017. Web.

———, "Let's Pretend."

———, "The Sacrifice."

———, "Snowrise"

———, "So This Is Good-Bye"

———, "Taylor's States." *Five 2 One Literary Journal*, 2017. Web.

———, "Uncle Hilbert's Cohens." *Atticus Review*, Feb. 2015. Web.

Williford, Lex, "The Coat." *Quarterly West* (1994); reprinted in *Sudden Flash Youth*, 2011.

Works Cited

Ackerman, Diane. *Deep Play*. New York: Random House, 1999.

Allen, Woody. "A Look at Organized Crime." *Getting Even*. Warner Paperback Library, 1971.

Anderson, Sherwood. *Winesburg, Ohio*, 1919.

Barthleme, Donald. "At the Tolstoy Museum." *City Life*. New York: Farrar Straus and Girous, 1970.

Boudinot, Ryan. "Cardiology." Originally published in *Five Chapters*; reprinted in *The Best Bizarro Fiction of the Decade*, ed. Cameron Pierce. Portland, OR: Eraserhead Press, 2012.

Brown, Randall, *Mad to Live*. Chico, CA: Flume Press, 2004.

Bunyan, John, *The Pilgrim's Progress*, 1687.

Delacroix, Eugene. *The Journal of Eugene Delacroix*. New York: Viking, 1972.

Dickens, Charles, *Sketches by Boz*, 1836.

Dinesen, Isak, "The Blue Jar." *Winter's Tales*, 1942.

Duck Soup [film, 1930]; excerpt from *The Essential Groucho: Writings by, for, and about Groucho Marx*, ed. Stefan Kanfer. New York: Vintage Books,2000.

Esquivel, Laura. *Like Water for Chocolate: A Novel in Monthly Installments, with Recipes and Home Remedies*. Trans. Carol Christensen and Thomas Christensen. New York: Doubleday, 1992.

Fisher, David. *Legally Correct Fairy Tales*. New York: Grand Central Publishing, 1996.

Fitzgerald, F. Scott. *The Crack-Up*. New York: New Directions, 1956.

Huizinga, Johan. *Homo Ludens: A Study of the Play Element in Culture* (1944); Boston: The Beacon Press, 1955.

Irving, Washington, *Salmagundi Papers*, 1807.

Keyes, Daniel. *Flowers for Algernon*. New York: Bantam Books, 1967.

Lightman, Alan, *Einstein's Dreams*. New York: Pantheon, 1993.

Maher, Bill. *The New New Rules: A Funny Look at How Everybody but Me Has Their Head Up Their Ass*. New York: Blue Rider Press, 2011.

Mahfouz, Naguib, "Dream #6" Trans. Raymond Stock; from *The Dreams*. Cairo: The American University in Cairo Press, 2000-2003;2004. Reprinted in *Flash Fiction International*, ed. James Thomas, Robert Shapard, and Christopher Merrill New York, W.W. Norton & Co., 2015.

Mason, Zachary, *The Lost Books of the Odyssey*. New York, Farrar Straus and Giroux, 2010.

Merwin, W.S., "A Fable of the Buyers," In *Imperial Messages: One Hundred Modern Parables*, ed. Howard Schwartz. New York: Avon Books, 1972.

Nutting, Alissa, "Hellion." In *Unclean Jobs for Women and Girls*. Reprinted in The *Best Bizarro Fiction of the Decade*, ed. Cameron Pierce. Portland, OR: Eraserhead Press, 2012.

Pascal, Blaise, *Lettres Provinciales*, 1657 [dedication page epigraph]

Perkins-Hazuka, Christine, Tom Hazuka, and Mark Budman, eds. *Sudden Flash Youth*. New York: Persea Books, 2011.

Phillips, Jayne Anne, "'Cheers,' (or) How I Taught Myself to Write." in *The Rose Metal Press Field Guide to Writing Flash Fiction*, ed. Tara L. Masih. Brookline, MA: Rose Metal Press, 2009.

Poe, Edgar Allan, Review of Nathaniel Hawthorne's *Twice-Told Tales*.

Rogers, Bruce Holland, "Aglaglagl." *The Sun*, Oct. 2010; reprinted in *Flash Fiction International*, ed. James Thomas, Robert Shapard, and Christopher Merrill New York, W.W. Norton & Co., 2015.

Shakespeare, William, *Hamlet* [dedication page epigraph]

Simon, Neil. *The Odd Couple*. New York: Random House, 1966.

Swift, Jonathan, "A Modest Proposal" (1729)

Unferth, Deb Olin, *Minor Robberies*. San Francisco: McSweeney's, 2007.

Villaverde, Athena. "Caterpillar." First published in *Clockwork Girl* 2011; reprinted in *The Best Bizarro Fiction of the Decade*, ed. Cameron Pierce. Portland, OR: Eraserhead Press, 2012.

Vonnegut, Kurt. *Slaughterhouse-Five*. New York: Delacorte, 1969.

White, Fred D. "Sentences," *Pleiades* 24.2 (2004).

Further Reading

Serious writers are also serious readers. To master the craft of flash fiction, one should read extensively in the genre, becoming familiar with its many varieties, and the virtuosity of its practitioners. Listed below is a comprehensive selection of anthologies devoted to flash fiction, noteworthy collections by individual authors, along with a sampling of the many periodicals that publish flash fiction.

Anthologies of Flash Fiction

The Best Small Fictions 2015, ed. Robert Olen Butler Queen's Fairy Press, 2015.

The Best Small Fictions 2016, ed. Stuart Dybek. Queen's Ferry Press, 2016.

The Best Small Fictions 2017, ed. Amy Hempel. Queen's Ferry Press, 2017.

Flash Fiction Forward, ed. James Thomas and Robert Shapard. Norton, 2006.

Flash Fiction International: Very Short Stories from Around the World, ed. James Thomas, Robert Shapard, Christopher Merrill. Norton, 2015.

Flash Fiction: 72 Very Short Stories, ed. Tom Hazuka et al. Norton, 1992.

Jawbreakers: A Collection of Flash-Fiction, ed. Calum Kerr and Valerie O'Riordan. Southampton, UK: Gumbo Press, 2012.

Micro Fiction: An Anthology of Fifty Really Short Stories, ed. Jerome Stern. Norton, 1996.

Scraps: A Collection of Flash-Fictions from National Flash-Fiction Day, 2013, ed. Calum Kerr and Holly Howitt. Southampton, UK: Gumbo Press, 2013.

Sudden Flash Youth: 65 Stories Featuring Young Protagonists, ed. Christine Perkins-Hazuka et al. Persea Books, 2011.

Sudden Flash Fiction: 65 Short-Short Stories, ed. Christine Perkins-Hazuka. Braziller, 2011

Anthologies of Short-Short Stories

Note: Short-short Stories are the next length-group up from flash—typically between 1100-2000 words. Some argue that, while lengthier, they possess the same aesthetic properties as flash fiction; but to me they lack the ultra-compression of flash. Of course, there is much overlap, so don't take the distinction between flash and short-short too seriously.

Microcosmic Tales: 100 Wondrous Science Fiction Short-Short Stories, ed. Martin H. Greenberg and Joseph D. Olander. DAW Books, 1980.

Playboy's Short-Shorts. The Editors of *Playboy*. Playboy Press, 1970.

Sudden Fiction, ed. Robert Shapard. Norton, 1983.

New Sudden Fiction: Short-Short Stories from America and Beyond, ed. Robert Shapard and James Thomas. Norton, 2007.

Anthologies of Short Humor

Russell Baker's Book of American Humor, ed. Russell Baker. Norton, 1993.

Flash Fiction Funny, ed. Tom Hazuka. Blue Light Press, 2013.

Individual Author Collections of Flash Fiction or Humor

Note: Several of these collections include longer stories as well as flash.

Woody Allen, *Getting Even*. Random House, 1970.

Richard Brautigan, *Revenge of the Lawn: Stories 1962–1970*. Simon & Schuster, 1971

Randall Brown, *Mad to Live* (Flume Press, 2008; PS Books 2011.

Italo Calvino, *Invisible Cities*. Trans. William Weaver. Harcourt Brace Jovanovich, 1974.

Raymond Carver, *What We Talk About When We Talk About Love*. Vintage, 1982.

Amy Clark, Elizabeth Ellen, Kathy Fish, Claudia Smith, *A Peculiar Feeling of Restlessness: Four Chapbooks of Short Short Fiction by Four Women*. Rose Metal Press, 2008.

Jackie Craven, *Our Lives Became Unmanageable*. Richmond, CA: Omnidawn Publishing, 2016.

Lydia Davis, *The Collected Stories of Lydia Davis*. Farrar Straus and Giroux, 2009.

Stuart Dybek, *Ecstatic Cahoots: Fifty Short Stories*. Farrar Straus and Giroux, 2014.

Sherrie Flick, *I Call This Flirting*. Flume Press, 2004.

Megan Giddings, *The Most Dangerous Game* (Lettered Streets Press, 2016.

Amelia Gray, *Museum of the Weird*. Fiction Collective 2, 2010.

Amy Hempel. *The Collected Stories of Amy Hempel*. Scribner, 2007

Etgar Keret, *The Nimrod Flipout*, translated by Miriam Shlesinger and Sondra Silverston. Farrar Straus and Giroux, 2006.

Tara Laskowski, *Modern Manners for Your Inner Demons*. Santa Fe Writers Project, 2017

Ben Loory, *Stories for Nighttime and Some for the Day*. Penguin Books, 2011.

Jeff Noon, *Pixel Juice. Stories from the Avant Pulp*. Doubleday, 1998

Bruce Holland Rogers, *The Keyhole Opera*. Wheatland Press, 2005.

Bob Thurber, *Nickel Fictions: 50 Exceedingly Brief Stories*. CreateSpace 2013.

James Thurber, *Fables for Our Time*, 1940.

Deb Olin Unferth, *Wait Till You See Me Dance: Stories*. Greywolf Press, 2017.

Joy Williams, *Ninety-Nine Stories of God*. Tin House Books, 2016.

Novels or Novellas Containing Flash Fiction Episodes

Note: The episodes in these novels form a coherent novel, but they can also stand alone.

Chris Bower, et al., *My Very End of the Universe: Five Novellas-in-Flash and a Study of the Form*. Rose Metal Press, 2015.

Jerzey Kosinski, *Steps*. Random House, 1969.

Alan Lightman, *Einstein's Dreams*. Pantheon Books, 1993

Zachary Mason, *The Lost Books of the Odyssey*. Farrar, Straus and Giroux, 2010.

Jennifer Tseng, *The Passion of Woo and Isolde*. Rose Metal Press, 2017.

Lex Williford, *Superman on the Roof*. Rose Metal Press, 2017.

Index

About the Author

Fred D. White received his Ph.D. in English from the University of Iowa, and taught courses in writing and literature in community colleges in Minnesota and, since 1980, at Santa Clara University in Northern California, where he is now professor of English, Emeritus. In 1996 he received the Louis and Dorina Brutocao Award for Teaching Excellence. Professor White has published several books on writing, as well as dozens of stories (many of them flash tales), essays, poems, and plays. He lives with his wife, Therese (an attorney), and their two cats, Emily and Otis, in Rancho Cordova, California.